STUDY GUIDE

THE NEW TESTAMENT

ROMANS TO CORINTHIANS

Freshly translated by Nicholas King

kevin mayhew

For Michael and Rachel, Jack and William, with love

First published in 2006 by
KEVIN MAYHEW LTD
Buxhall, Stowmarket, Suffolk, IP14 3BW
E-mail: info@kevinmayhewltd.com
www.kevinmayhew.com

The text for *Romans to Corinthians* first appeared in Nicholas King's translation of *The New Testament*.

9 8 7 6 5 4 3 2 1 0

ISBN 1 84417 546 4
Catalogue No. 1500899

Cover Design: Jonathan Stroulger
Editors: Peter Dainty, Marian Reid
Typesetting: Richard Weaver

Set in Simoncini Garamond and *Abadi MT Lt It*

Nihil Obstat: This translation has been examined by the Theology Committee of the Bishops' Conference of England and Wales and is declared free from doctrinal error. It is not authorised for use in the Liturgy of the Church and is approved for publication, in accord with Canon 825§1.

Mgr Andrew Summersgill, General Secretary, 8 June 2004

Printed and bound in Great Britain

Contents

Introduction

The key to understanding Paul is to remember all the time as you read that he had made the sudden and disconcerting discovery that it was all true about Jesus: Jesus was risen, Jesus had now to be worshipped as 'Lord', and he, Paul, now had a mission from Jesus to the non-Jews. This was a remarkable turn-around for one who had hitherto made it his mission to put an end to the claims of those who asserted that Jesus was alive. He went into it, however, with characteristic gusto, and with all the restless creativity of his intellect. One of the privileges that we have as we read Paul's letters is to watch his mind at work as he wrestles with the implications of this earth-shattering discovery and tries to talk business with the at times rather awkward members of the churches that he had founded.

It is true that some of the letters in the Pauline corpus (though not the three in the present volume) are judged by many scholars not to be from Paul's hand. These would include, in varying degrees of uncertainty, 2 Thessalonians, Ephesians, Colossians, 1 and 2 Timothy and Titus (although it has to be said that some scholars would make a case for all of these letters to have been written by Paul). Even if Paul did not write them, they are clearly evidence for the kind of thing that his immediate successors felt he would be saying 'if he were alive today'. And simply wrestling with the text and asking 'could Paul have written this?' is a useful discipline, which can teach us much about this prickly and passionate theological genius who was head over heels in love with Jesus.

One thing that it may be helpful to remember concerns the structure of letters in the ancient world. We tend to begin a letter with the name of the addressee ('Dear X'), and only put our name at the end ('Yours Ever, Fred', or whatever). In the ancient world (perhaps more logically) the author's name comes first, followed by greetings to the addressees, then a thanksgiving to the gods, followed by the main business of the letter, and finally the closing greetings. Paul always follows this pattern, except that in Galatians he is so cross that there is no thanksgiving. The difference is that Paul really makes the main body of the letter work for him; that is where he puts all the difficult theological argumentation. So Paul's letters are not exactly like other letters in the ancient world, but a creative improvement on the established practice to cope with the new reality that came into his life when he met Jesus.

Letters are always precious documents, because they tend to be intimate and personal, and Paul's letters are no exception to this rule. It is even true with regard to Romans, the most solemn and formal of all his epistles (and the only one written to a church that he had not founded). It is a diplomatic piece of writing, possibly intended to undo the damage caused by his intemperate remarks in Galatians. It is not, therefore, in my view, Paul's final treatment of matters theological (despite the influence it has exercised over the last five centuries). So readers should not worry if they do not readily grasp how all the arguments hang together. Paul does not, I think, always manage absolute coherence in his arguments. Instead of working it all out as a structured expression of his final theological position, try to see where Paul is going. And, I suggest, what Paul is about is a presentation of the basic question, 'What has God done in Christ Jesus?'. You might also read reflectively through chapter 16, which is never read in church, and consider why Paul lists all these names. What is he trying to say to the Roman Church?

In the two letters to Corinth which follow Romans, the argument is clearer: the Christians at Corinth were an impossibly divided group, and Paul is trying to put an end to the divisions. They were also, it seems, mistrustful of Paul, and a part of his task was to rebuild trust. Emotions run high in both of these letters, and it is good for us to know that such things can happen in the early church. Underneath the problems, try and get a feel for the way Paul operates, and admire his ability to 'think on his feet'. Paul was the 'great lover', whose love for Jesus turned the world upside down and whose experience of Jesus forced him to invent a new way of writing and talking. These three letters have much to tell you about that prickly and difficult character and about the two churches to which they are addressed, and much about what it was like to try to be a Christian in those years before people had settled into a way of being Christian; above all they have much to tell you about the one whom Paul knew as 'Lord', without whose Risen Presence none of them would have been written.

The Letter to the Romans

The Letter to the Romans

Romans is Paul's longest and most influential letter. It is also very hard going, and the translator faces a formidably difficult task. A single phrase in Romans 5:12, for example, may have as many as eleven different meanings, and the jury is still out on which of them best suits the context. Since, however, the aim of this translation is to persuade the reader 'back to the text', the measure of its success will be whether you are inclined to stop and ask: what is Paul saying to me, here and today? And behind what Paul may be saying (for he would have been very surprised to learn that we should still be reading his letters so many centuries later) is a further question: what is God saying? Or: what does all this have to do with the meaning of my life?

Some of the commentary sections are longer than I should wish. This is partly because of the difficulty of this epistle; you can ignore them if they do not help your reading.

Since the Old Testament is so important to the argument, I have given Paul's quotations from it in footnotes. Consult them if you think it will shed light on the argument.

At times, I have to say, I have despaired of making Romans intelligible to a modern reader who has not much acquaintance with the Christian tradition; but if you persevere, you will find this letter, though frustrating in places, enormously worth reading. What he has to say is worth saying, and needs to be heard today. It is our task to find language for it that makes some sense to those around us.

Introduction

1 1-7 Paul, a slave of Jesus Christ, called as an apostle set apart for the gospel of God, which [God] promised earlier through his prophets in the holy scriptures, about [God's] Son who came from the seed of David according to the flesh, who was marked out as Son of God, in power according to the Holy Spirit, as a consequence of the Resurrection [from the] dead, Jesus Christ our Lord, through whom we have received grace and a mission for faithful obedience among all the gentiles for the sake of his name. Among those Gentiles you too are called [to belong to] Jesus Christ – to all those who are in Rome, beloved of God, called [to be] saints, grace to you and peace from God our Father and the Lord Jesus Christ.

This opening to Paul's most difficult and most majestic epistle (and it feels more like an epistle than a letter, more a formal treatise than a scribbled note) is astonishingly dense. In Greek it is a single sentence. In certain moods, I imagine Paul roaring out his dictation of the letter, back in Corinth, with poor Tertius, his secretary for the occasion, struggling to keep up. In other moods, Romans reads like a very carefully planned document. As the letter continues we shall be looking for clues as to why he wrote it. For the moment, just get the feel of it.

The secret of the whole letter, and of the whole of Paul's Christian life, is in the opening four words (in Greek; they have to be six in English). There are, however, one or two other words and phrases that we need to keep an eye on:

- *'called . . . set apart': the mission is something thrust upon Paul, not something he has chosen for himself;*
- *'an apostle': this is an enormously important title for Paul. If ever you want to annoy him, just tell him that he is not a real apostle, because he persecuted the Church, and because he did not know Jesus in the days of his ministry;*
- *'the gospel of God': this is a very important phrase in Paul in general, and in Romans in particular. As you read through the document, try to build up your own understanding of the content of this gospel;*
- *'promised earlier through his prophets in the holy scriptures': central to Paul's theology (and it runs through the whole New Testament) is the certainty that the same God is at work in the Hebrew scriptures, in the life of Jesus, and in the Church's mission;*
- *'God's Son': Paul traces this a) through descent from David, and b) through what happened at the Resurrection. It is an important idea for Paul – try, as you read, to see what it means for him;*
- *'according to the flesh . . . according to the Holy Spirit [or: spirit of holiness]': this is the first mention of a contrast that will be important for the argument of Romans;*
- *'in power': another important idea for Paul. In his view, the message about Jesus makes a difference that you can feel;*
- *'Resurrection from/of the dead': for Paul, there is no gospel without Resurrection;*
- *'Jesus Christ our Lord': do not even try to count the number of times you will encounter this phrase in Paul. It is important to him, as naming the one he loves. Unlike the evangelists, Paul uses 'Christ' as a name, not a title. Calling him Lord means three things: First, Paul refers everything to Jesus and offers him unshakable allegiance. Second, he is using here 'Lord' language of Jesus, which until his life changed so dramatically he would have used only of God. Third, the word 'Lord' is a title that Roman emperors were now allowing to be used of themselves. A clash was inevitable;*
- *'grace and apostolic mission': we let these words go by almost without noticing; but they are of immense importance for Paul. 'Grace' means God's unconditional love for us, which is absolutely at the heart of his argument, and of Paul's dramatic change of life. 'Apostolic mission' is a consequence of what happened to him – his astonished discovery that God wanted him to tell non-Jews about this 'unconditional love' that God had shown in Jesus;*
- *'faithful obedience': this densely packed phrase includes 'obedience which consists in faith', 'obedience into faith', and 'obedience which springs from faith'. Don't try so much to understand as to experience it;*

- *'Among those Gentiles you too are called': the unconditional love is even on offer to non-Jews! And Paul delicately reminds the Roman Church that some of them (perhaps most of them) are in fact non-Jews;*
- *'beloved of God, called to be saints': this is not something that the Romans have achieved for themselves;*
- *'grace to you and peace from God our Father and the Lord Jesus Christ': a phrase of profound theological weight. It starts off looking like a regular formality of Greek correspondence – but there is nothing merely formal about God's unconditional love, nor about the 'peace' which only comes with God's gift of justice. As you read the letter, and the rest of Paul, you need to make up your mind about how Paul sees the relationship between 'God our Father' and 'the Lord Jesus Christ'. Here it seems that he holds them very nearly equal.*

CHAPTERS 1-4: FIRST MAIN SECTION – THE HUMAN PLIGHT AND GOD'S RESPONSE

Thanksgiving (or diplomatic tiptoeing?)

8-15 First of all, I thank my God through Jesus Christ with regard to all of you; because your faith is proclaimed in the whole world. For God is my witness (God whom I worship in my spirit and in the gospel of his Son) that unceasingly I make mention of you all the time in my prayers, begging that somehow, some time, at last I shall succeed in coming to you, by God's will. For I long to see you, in order that I might impart some spiritual gift to you, for you to be strengthened; [by] this means to receive some comfort with you, through our shared faith, yours and mine. I do not want you to be unaware, my fellow Christians, that I frequently intended to come to you – and up to this point I have been prevented – so that I might bear some fruit among you as among the rest of the Gentiles. I am under an obligation to Greeks and non-Greeks, to wise people and to fools – hence my eagerness to preach the gospel to you in Rome as well.

The thanksgiving is almost always a part of a letter from Paul, but look closely at the text here, and you will see that it is slightly perfunctory. What Paul is chiefly aiming to do, it seems, is to win them over. The Jerusalem Church and the Roman Church had links, so they will have heard about the fluttering in the dovecotes that had been caused by Paul's rather strong language in Galatians (despite its position in the New Testament, Romans was written after Galatians, and partly in an attempt to undo the damage). Paul did not found the Roman Church, but he wants to go there (as we learn also from Acts); and he wants to underline this desire of his. Why does he want to go there? He can hardly say that it is 'in order to preach the gospel to you', since they are already believers in Jesus; but he does hint at some such intention: 'to impart some spiritual gift to you, for you to be strengthened', before retreating from this position and making it more of a mutual preaching of the gospel. In the end, though, he is clear that evangelisation in Rome is his aim: 'that I might bear some fruit among you . . . to preach the gospel to you in Rome as well'. We shall not go far wrong if we think of him as treading on eggshells here.

Is Paul treading a tricky path here, do you think?

A summary of Paul's gospel?

16, 17 For I am not ashamed of the gospel. It is the power of God for the salvation of everyone who believes, whether Jew (in the first place) or Gentile. For God's Righteousness is revealed from faith to faith, as it is written, 'the just [person] shall live by faith'.

For many readers, these few lines summarise the whole epistle, and Paul's particular 'slant' on the gospel of Jesus Christ. The emphasis, all the time, is on what God has done, and it is 'power', something that they can see and feel. It is also unrestricted, no longer addressed exclusively to God's chosen race. It has to do with 'God's Righteousness' (and you must try to work out the meaning of this phrase as the letter unfolds. I capitalise it, to underline its importance in his thinking); it has to do with 'faith', perhaps 'beginning and ending in faith', and it is underpinned by the Habakkuk quotation that we shall hear again, 'the just person shall live by faith'.[1]

Why ***should*** *Paul be 'ashamed of the gospel'?*

The human plight

18-32 The wrath of God is revealed from heaven on all human impiety and unrighteousness, of those who hold back the truth by unrighteousness, because what may be known of God is revealed among them. For God revealed [it] to them. God's invisible attributes from the [very] creation of the world are understood, and perceived, by means of the things that God has made: I mean his personal power and divinity. The result is that they are without excuse; because they knew God, and yet failed to glorify God as such, or give thanks [to him]. Instead they were infatuated by their own thoughts, and their undiscerning heart was darkened. They told [everyone] that they were wise, but lapsed into folly. They swapped the glory of God Imperishable for a statue of a human being, or of birds, or quadrupeds, or creepy-crawlies!

For that reason, God handed them over to the desires of their hearts, to impurity, so that they dishonoured their own bodies with them. They swapped God's truth for falsehood; they gave worship and service to creatures, not to the Creator – Blessed be God for ever. Amen.

For that reason, God handed them over to degrading passions. For example, their womenfolk exchanged natural for unnatural sexual intercourse. Similarly the men abandoned natural sexual intercourse with women, and burnt with desire for each other: men committing disgusting deeds with other men, and receiving the inevitable penalty of their aberration.

1. Habakkuk 2:4

Just as they did not think it creditable to recognise God, God handed them over to a discreditable state of mind, [so as to do] things that are not fitting, filled with all kinds of unrighteousness, wickedness, greed, evil; filled with spite, murder, strife, treachery, malignity; whisperers, slanderers, God-haters, insolent overweening braggarts, inventors of evil, disobedient to their parents, unintelligent, undutiful, unloving, unmerciful. Such people, though they know perfectly well what God commands, and that people who do such things deserve to die, nevertheless don't just do them – they actually applaud those who act in this way!

We mop our brow upon reading this, and mutter 'Steady on, Paul; there are ladies present!', for he uses decidedly strong language; indeed, so powerful are his emotions that the syntax rather falls apart, as I have tried to convey in the translation. We need to keep our nerve, however, for he has a trick or two up his sleeve. In the first place, he is not so much describing what actually happens, as imagining The Worst. Second, he is leading us into a trap. So if you find yourself nodding your head in approval of his denunciation of contemporary morality, be careful, because he is going to turn on you ('anyone who judges') in the very next section. You might be encouraged in this restraint by noticing, third, that the list of vices is a fairly uneven one. It includes various kinds of homosexuality, but also lists idolatry of several sorts, as well as 'unintelligence . . . wickedness, greed . . . quarrelling . . . whispering . . . disobedience to parents'. Almost anything will do here to indicate the plight of human beings without God. We should read it as a picture of the loveless morass that we can drift into if we forget what we are made for.

And that, fourth, is the point. For Paul it is self-evident (in a way that it may not be to us) that homosexuality (and all the rest of the list) is something in which people get trapped through their own folly or failure, not an authentic expression of human love and goodness.

Finally, as always with Paul, especially in Romans, we have to see what he is really about. Paul is talking about God, and God's mercy on the mess that we have made. We have a long way to go in this letter, of course, but unless we see that central to its teaching is God's free gift, we shall simply have a lovely time condemning others, without recognising our own desperate need of God.

Do Christians find it too easy to condemn, do you think?

A terrible shock

2 1-11 So you have no excuse, my friend, whoever you are who judges. For on that precise point on which you judge your neighbour, you condemn your own self – for you who do the judging do the very same things yourself! We know that God's judgement is in truth on those who do such things. Is this what you think, my friend who judges those who do such things, and yet do them yourself, that you will escape from God's judgement? Or do you despise the riches of God's generosity, and clemency, and forbearance? Don't you realise that God's kindness is [meant to] lead you to repentance? But because of your hardness and unrelenting heart, you are storing

up a treasure-chest of wrath for yourself on the Day of the Wrath of God and the Day of the Revelation of God's Righteous Judgement, when 'he will repay each person in accordance with their deeds'. Some, because of their perseverance in good work [will receive] glory and honour and immortality – those who are seeking eternal life. Others, who are characterised by self-seeking, and who are disobedient to the truth and [instead] obey unrighteousness, will [receive] wrath and rage. Distress and anguish [will come] on the soul of every person who works evil – Jews first, and then Gentiles. Glory and honour and peace to everyone who works good – Jews first and then Gentiles. For there is no snobbery in God.

The reader here gets a salutary shock. When Paul says, 'So you have no excuse', we think that he is still getting after those Gentiles. Suddenly, though, and out of a clear sky, it is his Jewish readers who are on the receiving end, the very ones who had been saying 'I hope those Gentiles are listening to this.' As always, the key is the generosity of God, and it may help to remember that the two words that I have translated as 'generosity' and 'kindness' will have sounded in the Greek of Paul's day a bit like 'the Christ of God'. When Paul speaks of the Day of the Revelation of God's Righteous Judgement, it is important for us not to glance nervously at the calendar, in case it is falling due; instead we must focus on the mystery of who for Paul is 'righteous', and how.

A dense passage

12-16 For all those who have sinned outside the law will die outside the law. And those who have sinned under the law will be judged by the law. You see, it is not those who hear the law who are righteous before God; it is those who do the law who will be Regarded-as-Righteous.

For when Gentiles, although they do not get the law with their mother's milk, actually manage to do what the law prescribes, these people are their own law, even though they don't know the law. They demonstrate that the working of the law is written on their hearts; their conscience bears them witness, and among them their thoughts accuse them or even excuse them, on the day when God judges the things that human beings keep hidden, according to my gospel, through Christ Jesus.

This is a very tightly packed reflection on law and Being Righteous. It is not easy to translate the set of words associated with 'righteousness' or 'justification' in Paul, especially in Romans and Galatians; and his use of the word that I have translated as 'law' is not an easy one to put confidently and consistently into English. Perhaps at this stage the best thing is not to worry too much about the precise meaning but just get the 'feel', as you read the rest of the epistle, of the complex realities to which Paul refers. When he is obscure, it is sometimes better not to wrestle with him, but to move on.

Notice that towards the end of this passage a part of the intention of this letter surfaces, a defence of 'my gospel through Christ Jesus'. News of the ill-tempered confrontation in Galatia will have reached Rome, and Paul wants the Roman Christians to accept his own slant on the gospel of Jesus.

A question to reflect on throughout Romans: What is wrong with the law, according to Paul?

A difficult passage

17-24 If, however, you call yourself a Jew and rely on the law and boast in God; and if you know the will of [God], and discern what is best, because of having been instructed by the law you are convinced that you are a guide for the blind, and a light to those in darkness, and a tutor for those who can't think, a teacher for those who can't speak; [and if you think that you have] the embodiment of knowledge and truth in the law – do you then who teach your neighbour not teach yourself? Do you proclaim 'No Stealing' and yet steal? Do you tell [people] 'No Adultery' and commit adultery yourself? Do you abhor idols and [yet] rob temples? You who boast in the law, by your transgression of the law you dishonour God. For, as it is written, 'Because of you the name of God is blasphemed among the Gentiles.'

This is not easy; clearly Paul now has in his sights those Jews whom he imagined as criticising the Gentiles' disgraceful behaviour; but are we to suppose that he thought that all his fellow Jews were thieves, adulterers and temple robbers? All we can confidently say is that he wants them to hear, 'don't think you're safe'.

Real Judaism

25-29 For circumcision is useful, if you do [what] the law [commands]. If on the other hand you are a transgressor of the law, then your circumcision has become uncircumcision. So if uncircumcision keeps the law's commands, will not his uncircumcision be reckoned as circumcision? And [then] the [one who is] uncircumcised and who does the law will judge you who, for all your education and your circumcision, are a transgressor of the law. For it is not the one who is outwardly a Jew, nor the one who is outwardly circumcised, i.e. in the flesh, but the one who is a Jew in secret, and is circumcised in the heart, in spirit rather than in the letter, that is the one whose praise is not from human beings but from God.

This is another difficult passage; the point towards which he is working, however, does begin to emerge, that there is to be a new, and far less secure, definition of what it means to be a member of God's people. This is clearly something that Paul's Jewish readers are expected to find rather shocking.

What does Paul mean by 'circumcised in the heart'?

An imaginary dialogue

3 1-20 'In that case [you may want to ask], what advantage [does] the Jew have? How does circumcision help?'

[My Answer:] A great deal, in every way. For, Number One, they were entrusted with the oracles of God. You see, what if some have gone back on their trust, does their failure in trust undo God's trustworthiness? No way – let God be true, though every human were a liar, as it is written,

'So that you may be recognised as righteous by your words,
and you will be victorious when you are judged.'[2]

'Now if our unrighteousness serves to show God's righteousness, what shall we say? Can God who lets loose his anger be (humanly speaking) un-righteous?'

No way. For how will God judge the world?

'But if God's truth has redounded to his glory because of my falsity, why am I still being judged as a sinner?'

Surely it is not the case, as the slander against us goes, that (so some people allege) we do evil things so that good may come? These people deserve their condemnation.

'What then? Are we [Jews] superior?'

Not at all; for I have already charged that both Jews and all Gentiles are under sin, as it is written,

'There is no one righteous, not even one;
none who understands,
none who seeks God.
They have all turned aside, together they have become depraved.
There is none who does what is right,
not even one.'[3]
'An open grave is their throat;
with their tongues they have deceived.'[4]
'The poison of cobras is under their lips.'[5]
'Their mouth is full of cursing and bitterness.'[6]
'Their feet are swift to shed blood;
destruction and misery are in their way.'[7]
'And the way of peace they do not know
there is no fear of God before their eyes.'[8]

We know that whatever the law says, it speaks to those under the law, so that it might stop every mouth, and the whole world become liable to God's righteous judgement.

Therefore no human being shall be reckoned-as-righteous in his sight, for through the law [comes merely] consciousness of sin.

A difficult passage, and not really a dialogue at all, though it looks as though Paul is imagining possible objections to 'my gospel'. I have laid it out as a dialogue, however, so that you may see how it might have gone.

The two key ideas here are, first, the primary reality, which is God's righteousness, and, second, the human response, 'faith', or, as I have translated it in the second paragraph, 'trust'. When Paul says of his opponents that they

2. Isaiah 51:4
3. Psalm 14:1; Psalm 53:1-3
4. Psalm 5:9
5. Psalm 140:3
6. Psalm 10:7
7. Isaiah 59:7, 8
8. Psalm 36:1

'deserve their condemnation', and when he says of God that he 'will judge the world', the words used link with the idea of righteousness or justification. Paul also reiterates his important conviction that Jew and Gentile are on an equal footing in the face of God's judgement. He starts, moreover, at this point to hint at what is wrong (or insufficient) about the law. It is still only a hint, though, so we shall do well to withhold judgement until the end.

Why might Paul's first readers have been shocked at this idea of Gentiles and Jews being on an equal footing?

The heart of the matter: equality of all before God

21-26 As it is, God's righteousness has been revealed independently of law, although the law and the prophets testified to it; and God's righteousness, moreover, through Jesus Christ's faith [reaches out] to all who have faith. There is no distinction; for all have sinned and lack God's glory, reckoned-as-righteous at no cost, by his own free gift through the ransom [or: redemption] that took place in Christ Jesus. God offered Christ Jesus as a means of expiation, through faith, by his own blood, as a demonstration of his righteousness through the leaving unpunished of the sins that were committed in former times, by God's forbearance, to demonstrate his righteousness at the present time, so that he should be both righteous and righteous-maker, the one who is from Jesus' faith.

This is another densely packed passage, of which there are several interpretations. Rather than insist on one interpretation over against another (though I confess that translation is always already an interpretation) let me ask you to reflect on the following questions:

1. *What is the contrast between 'law' and 'righteousness of God'?*
2. *What is the meaning of 'faith of Jesus Christ'? Is it 'faith in Jesus' or 'the faith that Jesus showed'?*
3. *What does it mean to refer to Jesus as a 'means' (or 'place') of expiation?*
4. *Who is 'both righteous and righteous-maker'?*

The following ideas are clearly of importance here; work out for yourself how they come together:

- *God is just, and wants human beings to be so also.*
- *The scriptures tell us this.*
- *There are no 'front seats' in the theatre; all human beings have equal rights.*
- *Human sin is a reality that has to be dealt with. One metaphor for dealing with it is drawn from the slave-market. 'Ransoming' slaves ends up, via Latin, as 'redeeming' in English. Another metaphor is connected with the law courts, and means something like 'being acquitted', though it is more complicated than that. This is the idea that comes into English as 'justified' or 'made righteous'.*

Triumphant conclusion

27-31 So – what room is there for boasting? It is eliminated. On what kind of law? On the law of 'works'? No – on the law of 'faith'. For we calculate that a person is reckoned-as-righteous by faith, independently of works of the law.

Or [are you saying that] God is only [a God] for Jews? Surely God is God of the Gentiles also? Of course he is. For [it is] one [and the same] God who will reckon-as-righteous [both] the circumcised (as a result of faith) and the uncircumcised (through faith).

So – are we abrogating the law through faith? No way – on the contrary, we ***confirm*** the law.

It is evident from the tone here that Paul regards this as the successful culmination of his argument, but he leaves us trailing in his jet-stream, not without turbulence. Some key-ideas surface again here: law (which I have rather woodenly translated as such throughout, although occasionally 'principle' might be better here); faith; works; righteousness/justification. There is a final baffling rhetorical question about whether faith means the abrogation of law (which is what you might have supposed, up to this point), and which Paul now indignantly denies: 'we confirm the law'.

Perhaps the main thing to say, or rather to repeat, is that underlying all this is a question about God. And the heart of the matter is that there is not one God for Jews and another for Gentiles, but the same God for both.

In your own words, what do you understand Paul to be saying here about God?

A neat illustration

4 1-12 What then shall we say that Abraham found, our ancestor according to the flesh? If it was by [his] works that Abraham was reckoned-as-righteous, then he has grounds for boasting – but not before God. What does the scripture say? 'Abraham had faith in God, and it was reckoned to him as righteousness' – but if someone is working, his wages are not reckoned as a 'freebie', but as something he is owed. Whereas if someone is not working, but has faith in the One who 'reckons-the-godless-as-righteous', then his faith is reckoned to him as righteousness.

In just the same way, David also speaks a blessing over the person to whom God has reckoned righteousness independent of works:

'Blessed are those whose lawlessness is forgiven
and whose sins are covered.
Happy the one whose sins God does not reckon up.'[9]

Now – is this blessing [called down] on the circumcised or the uncircumcised? For we say 'his faith was reckoned to Abraham as righteousness'. So how was it reckoned? When he was circumcised or when he was uncircumcised? Not when he was circumcised, but when he was uncircumcised. And he took the sign of circumcision as a seal

9. Psalm 32:1, 2

of the righteousness-by-faith which [he received while he was still] uncircumcised – so that he is the ancestor of all those who believe through uncircumcision, so that righteousness-is-reckoned to them also; and he is the ancestor of all those who have faith through uncircumcision, so that it is reckoned-to-them-as-righteousness, and the ancestor of circumcision for those who don't just depend on circumcision, but who also follow in the footsteps of the faith that our ancestor Abraham had when he was still uncircumcised.

This is still not particularly easy, but the general lines of the argument are perhaps becoming clearer to the reader. Paul adopts a rather neat way of arguing. He takes the example of Abraham, whom all Jews revere as their ancestor; and he argues that Abraham is also the ancestor of uncircumcised Gentiles! Why? Remember that Paul is arguing that Gentiles who become Christians do not need to fulfil requirements of the Jewish law, such as circumcision, but they have been given righteousness-by-faith, which Paul contrasts with 'righteousness-from-observing-the-law'. But Abraham, he shrewdly points out, had righteousness attributed to him because of his faith as early as Chapter 15 of Genesis, whereas he is not circumcised until Chapter 17.

So Abraham had not done anything, only responded to God's love; certainly he had not observed the Torah at this stage – and yet he was made 'father of many nations', which in Greek is the same as 'father of many Gentiles', as many as the stars of the heaven or the sands of the seashore.

Still finding it difficult? Don't worry – read on.

Paul's explanation

13-17 For it was not through law that the promise came to Abraham or to his seed, [the promise of] inheriting the world; that promise came through 'righteousness-by-faith'. You see, if the law-dependent people inherit, then faith is emptied of content, and the promise is abrogated. Because the law brings about wrath; whereas where there is no law, there is no transgression.

Hence the 'from faith' bit, so that it would be according to God's-unconditional-gift, so that the promise would be sure for 'all his seed', not just for the Abraham who was law-dependent, but for the Abraham who depended on faith, who is the ancestor of us all, as it is written, 'I have made you the ancestor of many nations [or Gentiles]',[10] in the sight of the God in whom he trusted, [the God] who makes the dead alive, and calls that which is non-existent into existence.

Still puzzled? It may help to notice how Paul's attention is exclusively on God. One difficulty that you may still feel is how 'the law brings about wrath': as you read through the rest of this chapter you can ask whether he manages to answer this question, which is obviously important for the working of his argument. Paul does not perhaps trouble too much about the steps of the argument, since he has already long since arrived at the conclusion, which is

10. Genesis 17:5

that God has given us as a free gift the not-guilty verdict that the law failed to achieve. To receive the free gift, humans have only to respond (like Abraham) in faith. Then even the deadness of Abraham and the deadness of Jesus is no longer an obstacle to the power of God's love.

Why was Abraham important for Paul's argument?

The conclusion

18-25 So [Abraham], hoping against hope, made-an-act-of-faith that he [could] become the father of many nations [or Gentiles], according to what had been said, 'So [i.e. according to the number of the stars] shall your seed [or descendants] be.'[11] And Abraham did not weaken in faith when he considered the deadness of his own body (for he was about a hundred years old) and the deadness of Sarah's womb. In the face of God's promise, he was not in doubt through lack-of-faith; instead, he was empowered through faith, and gave glory to God, and was fully convinced that what [God] had promised, God was capable also of putting into action. Therefore 'it was reckoned to him as righteousness.'[12] Now this 'it was reckoned' was not written just for him, but also for us, to whom it is going to be 'reckoned', us who believe in the One who raised Jesus Our Lord from the dead, Jesus who was handed over on account of our sins, and was raised up on account of our righteous-making.

So this difficult argument comes gently into harbour, and the reader may be glad to know that the hardest part of Romans is behind us. The key to not being driven mad by the argument is to recall that Paul always has his eye on the destination, what God has ready for those who believe, and is a bit casual in his description of the voyage itself, perhaps because it seemed so obvious to him. Paul is obsessed by God and by Christ, and by what God has done in Christ, and wants nothing else to get in the way (such as circumcision, law, 'works'). God has given believers a free gift that in no way depends on anything we can do for God, and demands only the loving response that Paul calls 'faith' or 'trust' or 'commitment'.

What does Paul mean by 'faith'?

CHAPTERS 5-8: SECOND MAIN SECTION – REASONS FOR HOPE

Paul has now got the difficult bit out of the way (though not all of what follows is going to be plain sailing). We may not have understood every step of his journey so far, but clearly the heart of the matter is that what God does for us or offers to us is not dependent on what we deserve or achieve, but on God's 'free gift', for which Paul has used metaphors from the slave market ('ransomed/redeemed') and from the law court ('acquitted/reckoned-as-righteous'). Our response is to be that commitment and trust which Paul calls 'faith'. The importance of this is that non-Jews, to whom Paul feels especially

11. Genesis 15:5
12. Genesis 15:6

called, don't have to observe all the details of Torah, if they are to respond to what God has done in Christ. For such people, Abraham acts (rather surprisingly) as a kind of icon, because he showed his faith before his circumcision took place. Now read on.

God's unbelievable generosity in Christ

5 1-11 So we have been reckoned-as-righteous as a result of [our] faith. We have peace with God through Jesus Christ, through whom we have gained access by faith to this free gift in which we stand, and boast in [the] hope of the glory of God.

Not only that; but let us also boast of our afflictions, knowing that affliction brings about steadfastness, and steadfastness brings about character, and character brings about hope. And hope does not disappoint, because the love of God is poured out in our hearts through the Holy Spirit that is given us.

You see, Christ, when we were still weak, nevertheless died at the right time on behalf of the impious!

Now you ***might**** just about die for a righteous person [literally, 'for with difficulty someone will die on behalf of a just man'].

Perhaps a person might have the guts to die in a good cause.

But God demonstrates his own love for us, in that while we were still sinners, Christ died on our behalf!

How much more, then, now that we have been reckoned-as-righteous by his blood, shall we be saved through him from the wrath? For if when we were [his] enemies we were reconciled to God through the death of his Son, how much more, now that we have been reconciled, shall we be saved by his life?

Not only that, but we actually boast in God through our Lord Jesus Christ through whom we have now received reconciliation.

In the three chapters that follow, Paul abandons the polemical tone and the slightly impenetrable argumentation that we have grappled with hitherto. Now he is trying to offer the grounds for hope. The reasoning is that a) we have peace with God; b) this peace comes for free; c) difficulties of various kinds do not count against this peace; d) God's gift in Christ is given to the undeserving; e) the icing on the cake is Jesus' resurrection: not just his generous death, but also the conquest of death.

Adam and Christ contrasted: the catastrophe reversed (and then some!)

12-21 Because of this, just as through one human being sin entered the world, and through sin death [entered the world], and so death came to all human beings seeing that all sinned.

For before law, sin was in the world; sin [could] not be charged to our account while law did not yet exist. Nevertheless, death was sovereign from Adam to Moses,

* Words in bold throughout the text are my emphasis

even over those who had not sinned, in the likeness of the transgression of Adam, who is the 'type' of the One who is to come.

BUT the free gift doesn't simply balance out the original transgression.

The thing is, many people died because of that one man's transgression, and all the more God's grace, and the free gift by the grace of that one man Jesus Christ, [simply] overflowed to the many.

And the gift was not just a consequence of one man having sinned. For the judgement, arising out of that one man, issues in a verdict of 'guilty', and the free gift that arose out of many transgressions issued in a verdict of 'not guilty'.

Now – if because of the one man's transgression death reigned through that one man, how much more will those who have received the abundance of grace and the free gift of righteousness, rule, through the one man Jesus Christ!

So then, it goes like this: just as the result of that one man's transgression issued in a verdict of 'guilty' on all human beings, so one man's righteousness issued in a verdict of 'not guilty' [or: acquittal, righteousness] and of life.

[To put it another way]: just as that single man's disobedience resulted in many peoples being made sinners, so, because of that other man's obedience, those many people are made righteous [or: not guilty].

And then law sneaked in, to increase the transgression. But where sin increased, grace was present in even greater abundance, so that:

just as sin ruled by means of death
so grace should rule through righteousness
and lead to everlasting life, through Jesus Christ Our Lord.

Once again Paul brings the difficult argument to a smooth end with that gentle and entirely characteristic conclusion, 'through Jesus Christ Our Lord'. But as we look back we can see the shape of the argument. First he makes a contrast between the powers: sin-guilt-death against obedience-righteousness-life where righteousness is the 'not guilty' verdict, and life is the idea, all-important to Paul, of resurrection.

Second, the phrases 'all the more' and 'how much the more', which appear three times in the first part of Chapter 5, remind us that it is not a simple contrast between Adam and Christ; God's response to our plight is one of overwhelming generosity that reverses the catastrophe, and then a whole lot more. At times in this section, the thought may cross the reader's mind that Paul is so excited that he can hardly dictate coherently.

What is the difference between Adam and Christ, for Paul?

A possible objection answered

6 1-11 'What shall we say then? Are we to persist in sin, so that grace may be on the increase?'

No way! Given that we have died to sin, how shall we continue to live in it? Or don't you realise that we who were baptised into Christ Jesus were baptised into his death? So through [our] baptism we were buried with him into death, so that just as

Christ was raised from the dead by the Father's glory, so we also should walk in newness of life.

You see, if we have 'grown together' in the likeness of his death, then we shall also 'grow together' in the likeness of his resurrection. So we know that our 'old humanity' has been crucified along with [Jesus], so that the sinful body is destroyed, with the result that we are no longer in slavery to sin. For the one who has died has been justified from sin.

If we have died with Christ, we have faith that we shall also live with him. We know that because Christ was raised from the dead he does not die any more: death no longer exercises its Lordship over him. You see, [the death] which he died, he died to sin – once and for all – whereas [the life] which he lives, he lives for God. So you [must all] reckon yourselves as dead to sin, but alive to God – in Christ Jesus.

Paul starts this portion off with another of his rhetorical questions, perhaps an objection from an imaginary opponent. The answer he gives enables him to do three things:

1. *He makes the contrast between our plight and what God in Christ has done for us (from death to life);*
2. *he links the Romans' experience of their own baptism to this contrast (from death to life);*
3. *he asserts the absolute centrality, for Jesus, and then for all Christians, of the Resurrection (from death to life).*

The whole story, for Paul, is one of movement from one power (sin-death) into another power (life-resurrection). So he is expressing in another way the contrast made in the previous chapter between what Adam did and what Jesus did.

Let God rule, not sin and death

12-14 Therefore:

- don't let sin rule in your mortal body, so that you obey sin's passions;
- don't give over your limbs as weapons of unrighteousness for sin;
- but do give yourself over to God, like people who are alive after death.

And do give your limbs over as weapons of righteousness for God. Sin does not Lord it over you; for you are not under the law, but under God's free gift.

Just at the end there, Paul raises once again the problem of the relationship of law and sin. Try, as you read, to ask the question, 'What, for Paul, is wrong with the law?' It may be helpful to notice the almost feudal idea of one's limbs as weapons offered in the service of a higher authority.

Notice also the wide range of ideas collected under the verb that I have translated as 'Lord it over': this includes the following:

- *language hitherto reserved in Jewish culture for God;*

- *language that was now increasingly being used for the Roman Emperor, which was therefore an alternative power;*
- *language applied to Jesus, in an increasingly exalted way.*

Another specious argument answered: the battle of the powers

15-23 'What then: are we to sin [seeing] that we are not under the law, but under grace?'

No way – don't you know that if you present yourselves as slaves, with a view to obedience, you are slaves to that which you obey, whether that is sin that leads to death, or obedience that leads to life. Thanks [or: grace] be to God, because you were slaves of sin; but you obeyed wholeheartedly in accordance with the pattern to which you have been committed: you have been set free from sin and 'enslaved' to righteousness.

I am speaking in human terms, because of the weakness of your [frail] humanity. So, just as you presented your limbs as slaves to impurity and lawlessness to achieve iniquity, so now present your limbs as slaves to righteousness to achieve holiness. For when you were slaves to sin, you were free with regard to righteousness. And so what fruit did you have then? [Things] of which you are now thoroughly ashamed – for these things end up in death.

As it is, you have been freed from sin, and 'enslaved' to God; you have your fruit [which leads] to holiness – and that ends up in eternal life. For the wages of sin is death; whereas God's free gift is eternal life in Christ Jesus Our Lord.

Once again, Paul poses an objection from an imaginary opponent, raising the spectre that sin might be a good thing; once again, he comes safely into harbour, concluding his argument 'in Christ Jesus Our Lord'. (Sometimes it seems that Paul cannot write a sentence without mentioning Jesus!) The basic answer, however, has to do with the clear sense of a battle between two opposing powers: death and life. One difficulty here is that Paul does occasionally use the same word in more than one meaning. For example, the word translated here as 'thanks' is his normal word for 'grace', a key idea in Romans; and in the same sentence I have had to translate one word both as 'lawlessness' and as 'iniquity'. Likewise I have put 'enslaved' in speech marks, because for Paul the believer's relationship to God is in principle quite different from that which people have to 'impurity and lawlessness'.

Are Christians 'enslaved' to God?

The problem of the law – an illustration

7 1-6 Or are you unaware, my brothers and sisters (for I speak to those who know the law), that the law lords it over the human being for as long as he or she is alive?

Let me give you an example: the married woman is bound by law to her husband while he is alive. If he dies, however, she is then released from the law [that binds her to] her husband. While her husband is alive, therefore, she is called an 'adulteress' if she belongs to another man; if, however, her husband dies, she is free of his law, so that she isn't an adulteress if she belongs to another man.

In just the same way, my brothers and sisters, you too have died to the law through the body of Christ, so that you belong to Another, the One who was raised from the dead, in order that we might bear fruit for God. For when we were in the 'flesh', the sinful passions which come through the law are at work in our limbs – so that they bear fruit for death. As it is, we are released from the law; we have died to that by which we were subjugated, so that we live a new sort of 'slavery', that of the Spirit, not the old sort, that of the letter.

Paul is here seeking to explain his 'gospel of freedom' by an illustration from marital law: just as the wife is no longer bound to her husband when he dies, so the individual is freed by death from the law. You can see what Paul is getting at – but the death in the case of the believer is of course that of Jesus Christ, which slightly unbalances the illustration.

Paul uses here and elsewhere the contrast between 'flesh' and 'spirit'. One helpful way of looking at this may be to think of 'flesh' as humanity when closed to God, and 'spirit' as humanity when it is open to God. This latter use is connected to, but also distinct from, Paul's use of the term 'Holy Spirit'.

Two more Jewish objections answered

7-13 'What shall we say, then? Does this mean that law is sin?'

No way – nevertheless, I only know sin through law. For I should not have known desire if the law had not said, 'Thou shalt not desire.'[13] Sin took its opportunity from the commandment and called forth all kinds of desire in me. For without law, sin is dead. I was once alive, independent of law; then when the commandment came sin sprang to life, but I died, and it turned out in my case that the commandment that was supposed to lead to life was the very one that led to death. For sin took its opportunity; through the commandment sin cheated me, and through it sin killed me.

[My conclusion is] that the law is holy, and the commandment is holy, and righteous, and good.

'Does that mean that the good for me became death [for me]?'

No way – what happened was that sin [became death to me]. In order that sin might appear, [as sin], sin brought about death [to me] through what was good for me, in order that sin might become exceedingly sinful through the commandment.

Paul is still wrestling with this desperately difficult question of the relationship of sin and law. In certain moods, the idea that law brings about sin can seem mysterious to us; in other moods, we know the contrary effect that the words 'thou shalt not' can have on us.

13. Exodus 20:17; Deuteronomy 5:21

We must never lose sight of Paul's main contention: there is a battle between death and life, and only God's free gift in Jesus Christ can put us on the side of life. One answer that is sometimes given to the question 'What is wrong with the law for Paul?' is that 'It's not Jesus Christ'.

The plight of sinners

14-23 You see – we know that the law is spiritual, whereas I am flesh, sold in bondage to sin, and I [hardly] know what I am doing. What I want to do is not what I [succeed in] doing; what I loathe is what I [end up] doing! Now, when I do what I do not want to do, I agree with the law, that it is good. And so in this case it is no longer I that am at work, but [the power of] sin that dwells in me.

I know, you see, that no good dwells in me (that is, in my flesh [my humanity as not open to God]). For I find it easy to will what is good; but actually to do it – not at all! For I don't [manage to] do the good that I want to do; instead it is evil, which I don't want to do, that I end up performing.

But if I'm doing what I don't want to do, it is no longer I who am at work, but the sin that dwells in me.

So this is the principle that I have discovered: when I want to do what is morally good, it is easy for me to do evil. For in my inner self, I joyfully resonate with God's law; but there is another law that I see in my limbs, which is at war with my mind's law, and keeps me imprisoned by the law of sin which is in my limbs.

Paul is still struggling with the question of how sin and law are related; and perhaps we can only follow his argument occasionally. This passage includes what feels at times like Paul's own personal experience; many Christians have been encouraged by the thought that Paul too struggled to do what he knew to be right. Some scholars argue, however, that Paul's use of 'I' is here intended to capture the experience of those who live the old life, not his present experience of living in the new life of Christ.

As always, that is the unfailing direction of his argument, and now this portion of the text comes to a stirring conclusion: the answer is Jesus Christ.

When Paul speaks of 'I' in this passage, is he telling his own story, or that of people without Christ?

Jesus is the answer

24, 25 What wretched human beings we are! Who will deliver us from this body of death? Thanks to God through Jesus Christ our Lord. To sum up: with my mind I am a slave of God's law; but in my unregenerate humanity, I am a slave of the law of sin.

Once again the reader asks: Is Paul talking about himself (and clearly Paul was not perfect) or about the plight of human beings without Christ? Turn the argument the other way round, though, and perhaps it does not matter: the solution for every problem that faces us, whether Paul or me or you, is Christ. So Paul, struggling through his argument, shouts (though not as loudly as he will soon be shouting) 'Thanks [or: 'grace'] to God!'

What has God done for us in Christ?

8 1-8 In conclusion, then, there is no condemnation for those who are in Christ Jesus: the law of the Spirit (i.e. life in Christ) has freed you from the law of sin and death.

What the law was incapable of, because of its weakness, through the flesh, God achieved. God sent his own Son, in the likeness of sinful flesh; and to atone for Sin, God condemned Sin in the flesh, so that the decree of the law might be fulfilled in us who behave, not according to the flesh [humanity closed to God], but according to the Spirit [humanity open to God].

For those who live according to the flesh are flesh-minded; those who live according to the Spirit are Spirit-minded. For flesh-thought is death, whereas Spirit-thought is life and peace.

Because flesh-thought is hostility towards God, it doesn't obey the law of God – it can't. Those who are in the flesh are incapable of pleasing God.

> *We stumble along after Paul; this is not really our thought-world. Nevertheless, we can keep our eyes on the main point: the battlelines are drawn between spirit and flesh, life and death. God in Christ has given us the opportunity of doing what we could not do for ourselves, ending up on the right side in the conflict.*
>
> *What do you think that 'flesh' means in these passages?*

What the Spirit does

9-11 You, however, are not in the flesh, but in the Spirit, if indeed the Spirit of God dwells among you. If, however, someone does not have the Spirit of Christ, that person does not belong to [Christ]. If Christ is in you, then, while the body may be dead because of sin, the Spirit is life because of righteousness. If the Spirit of the One who raised Jesus from the dead dwells among you, the One who raised Christ from the dead will also give life to your mortal bodies through his Spirit that dwells among you.

> *Once again, we are aware of two worlds: the world of death and the world of the Spirit; but here Paul's emphasis is on what the Spirit can do. We notice again, as so often in Paul, the central position that he gives to the Resurrection.*
>
> *At this point the reader may also want to start asking 'Who is the Spirit?'*

What the Spirit gives

12-17 So, brothers and sisters, we are under obligation – but not to the flesh, to live according to the flesh. For if you live according to the flesh, you're going to die, whereas if in the Spirit you put to death the doings of the body, you will live. You see, whoever are led by the Spirit of God, these are the ones who are children of God; for you did not receive the spirit of slavery, [to fall] back into fear – you received the spirit of adoption-as-sons, which causes us to cry out, 'Abba, Father'. The Spirit testifies in support of our spirit, that we really are children of God. Now if we are children, then we are also heirs, heirs of God, and co-heirs with Christ, if we have joined in his passion in order to join also in his glory.

From speaking of two realms, Paul moves almost imperceptibly into talking of only one realm. He starts this part by speaking of 'flesh' and 'death', but soon moves into that other realm, of the Spirit, and what the Spirit gives: the move out of slavery, and fear, and death into freedom, or what I had to translate 'adoption-as-sons' (even though it applies equally to woman believers). The situation from which Paul draws this underlying image is that of the Roman and Greek household, in which the eldest son was normally the heir; and although there would be slaves in the same household, there would ordinarily be no question of their inheriting. But adoption was a very common device, so that the father of the house should not die childless, and those who might be adopted could include either slaves of one's own house or children of another family. 'Adoption' is now the third image that Paul has used in Romans for what God has done for us in Christ, after 'acquitting' and 'ransoming'. It links closely with Jesus' frequent presentation of God-as-Father, which reaches its striking climax in Mark's account of Gethsemane, with the cry, to which Paul here alludes, of 'Abba, Father'. This cry for Christians signifies a new life and undeserved status.

Why did the early Christians remember that Jesus addressed God as 'Abba'?

Looking ahead to God's gift

18-30 For I reckon that the sufferings of the present epoch are not worth balancing against the glory that is about to be revealed to us. You see, the eager expectation of the creation is awaiting the revelation of the children of God. For the creation became subject to frustration, not by its own volition, but because of the One who had subjected it in hope. Creation itself will also be set free ***from*** the slavery of decay ***for*** the freedom of the glory of God's children.

We know, don't we, that the whole of creation groans and suffers labour pains together right up to the present moment. Not only that, but those who have the Spirit's first fruits, that is we ourselves, groan inside ourselves, waiting for our adoption-as-sons, waiting for the redemption of our bodies.

We were saved in hope: now a hope [whose object] can be seen isn't hope [at all], for who 'hopes' for something they can actually see? But if we are hoping for what we [can't] see, then we are waiting patiently.

In just the same way, the Spirit comes to the aid of our weakness. We have no idea what to pray for in the proper way; instead the Spirit itself pleads on our behalf, with wordless groans. The one who searches hearts knows what is the thought of the Spirit, because according to God's will the Spirit prays for the saints.

We know that for those who love God, everything cooperates to bring about good; those are the ones who are also called according to [God's] purpose: those whom he knew in advance, he also decided upon in advance as being like his son, so that he is the first-born among many brothers and sisters. Those whom he decided upon in advance [are] the ones he also called; and those whom he called, are the ones whom he reckoned-as-righteous; and those whom he reckoned-as-righteous are the ones whom he also glorified.

Paul, in this long section that has run from the beginning of Chapter 5, has been trying to give us grounds for hope. The invitation here is to look into a future that we can't quite see, and therefore have to hope for. Paul's tactic is to encourage us to hope by lifting our gaze from the present upwards into God's plan. The present finds us 'groaning' and 'frustrated'; but thanks to the Spirit we can look ahead to God's incomprehensible dispensation. This is good news for those whom God has chosen; they are the ones whom Paul is trying to encourage here. His attention is at this point not at all on people who have not responded to God; so there is no room here for the dreadful doctrine of 'double predestination' ('I'm in and you're out') that has caused so much trouble in my country of South Africa. This passage is for our encouragement, not for anyone else's discouragement.

What is the 'good news' here?

A glorious conclusion

31-34 So what shall we say to this? If God is on our side, who is against us? God [you remember] did not spare his own son, but handed him over on behalf of all of us – how can he help but give us everything as a free gift, along with him [the greatest of God's gifts]? Who shall bring charges against God's chosen ones? God is the One who reckons-as-righteous – who is the condemner? Christ Jesus is the one who died, and – more than that – was raised!

He is the one who is at God's right hand.
He is the one who intercedes for us.

We may not have followed the argument all the way, but we cannot help being buoyed up by the lyrical certainty of Paul's optimism as (once again) we come gently into harbour after the rough seas of some decidedly tricky argument.

A 'purple passage'

35-39 Who shall separate us from Christ's love?

Affliction? Anguish? Persecution? Famine? Nakedness? Danger? Execution? As it is written:

'For your sake we are done to death all day [long].
We are Reckoned as sheep for the slaughter.'[14]

No – in these matters we are winning a most glorious victory through the one who loved us. I am persuaded, you see, that neither death nor life, nor angelic nor demonic rulers, nor present nor future events, nor powers, nor height nor depth, nor

14. Psalm 44:22

any other created thing, will be able to separate us from the love of God, which is in Christ Jesus our Lord.

This is one of those 'purple passages' that enable the critical reader to forgive Paul all his prickliness and the numbing obscurity of some of his arguments. We may not understand quite how the arguments work, nor what precisely are the threats that Paul refers to, which might 'separate us from Christ's love', but there is no mistaking his confidence at the end, with that final phrase, so characteristic of Paul, so very much at the heart of this great lover: 'the love of God, which is in Christ Jesus our Lord'.

Is it accurate to call Paul a 'great lover'?

CHAPTERS 9-11: THIRD MAIN SECTION – WHAT ABOUT PAUL'S FELLOW JEWS?

The story so far: Paul has worked out a heavily scriptural argument to defend 'his gospel', that what God has done for us is God's free gift, and therefore does not depend on anything we can do, including having ourselves circumcised. In the second section, he showed why non-Jews who are committed to faith in Christ have grounds for hope. That, however, leaves unanswered the question of God's Chosen Race. This was an existential question for Paul, who never ceased to regard himself as a Jew, and for many of his Roman readers, several of whom will have been Jewish.

How do Jews fit into God's plan?

9 1-5 It is the truth that I am speaking in Christ. I am not lying; my conscience bears me witness in the Holy Spirit – I have a great grief, and a constant pain in my heart. For my prayer was to be accursed and [separated] from Christ for the sake of my brothers and sisters, my fellow Jews according to the flesh.

They are Israelites. Theirs is the adoption-as-children, and the glory, and the covenants, and the law-giving, and the cult, and the promises. Theirs are the ancestors. From them came the Messiah, according to the flesh, the one who is God over all, blessed for ever. Amen. [Or, with a different punctuation of the Greek: 'May God who is over all be blessed for ever. Amen.']

You may make a number of objections to Paul; one thing, however, that you cannot say of him is that he is a liar. You can hear the sincerity in his voice as he contemplates the possibility of being cut off from his beloved Christ in order to have his fellow Jews take up their rightful place in God's dispensation. Christians, with our embarrassing and wholly unjustified tradition of anti-Semitism, need to listen carefully to Paul as he lists all the assets that his fellow-Jews have: the privilege of being Israel, of being 'sons-and-daughters-of-God', of being the spectators (at Sinai, presumably) of the glory of God, of having received the covenants (at least those to Abraham and to Moses), having had the privilege of being told how to worship (in the tent and in the

Temple), who gave the world the Twelve Patriarchs, and, best of all for Paul, who produced Jesus Christ.

Notice the very different, far less negative, sense of 'flesh' here when Paul speaks of his fellow Jews as his 'kinsfolk according to the flesh' and of Christ as having come from the Jews 'according to the flesh'.

The final sentence of this portion might, if you punctuate it in one way, be a rare explicit reference on Paul's part to Christ as God. Punctuate it another way, and it becomes an 'arrow prayer' of praise to God for the excellence of the divine dispensation.

What is so special about the Jews, in Paul's view?

Just are the ways of God

6-13 Of course, it is not the case that God's word has failed. For not all those descendants of Israel are [real] Israel. Nor is it the case that all who are physically descended from Abraham are in fact his children. No – 'from Isaac physical descendants shall be called [forth] for you'.[15]

What this means is not that the children of the flesh really are children of God, but that the children of the promise are reckoned-as-descendants. For this is how the promise is expressed: 'At this time I shall come, and Sarah shall have a child.'[16]

Not only that: Rebecca conceived [children] by one man, Isaac our ancestor. When they were not yet born, and had not done anything good or evil, so that God's purpose of election might be assured, not by works but by the one who issues the invitation, she was told 'the older one will be a slave to the younger one',[17] as it is written, 'I loved Jacob and hated Esau.'[18]

One thing Paul has to do here is to demonstrate to his Jewish readers (and his reference to 'Isaac our ancestor' makes it clear that it is they whom he has in mind here) that God has not gone back on his promise. One of the ways of managing this is to argue that it was all foreshadowed in Scripture, which, for Paul, is God's dictated word; and so he is able to use texts that point a) to Abraham as the father of many 'Gentiles' and b) to the unexpectedness of God's election, as when of Isaac's two children the older is placed after the younger. Underneath all that, of course, is God's sovereign freedom to do exactly as he pleases. Like a 400lb-gorilla.

Once again you can see how later readers of Paul built on what he writes here, about the 'children of the flesh' over against the 'children of the promise', the dreadful doctrine of 'double predestination'. Once again, though, it is necessary to remind ourselves that Paul's interest is in the positive, 'what God has done in Christ', not the negative, 'those who are beyond God's love'. For Paul, no one is beyond God's love.

Why does Paul mention Jacob and Esau here?

---

15. Genesis 21:12
16. Genesis 18:10
17. Genesis 25:23
18. Malachi 1:2, 3

Two more imaginary objections answered: God is not unjust, but merciful

14-23 'What shall we say then? Surely there is no unrighteousness in God?'

No way – he tells Moses: 'I shall have mercy on the one on whom I shall have mercy, and I shall pity the one whom I shall pity.'[19] It is not therefore a matter of [human] will or of [human] exertion [literally: running], but of God's mercy. For Scripture tells Pharaoh, 'For this very reason I have raised you up, so that I may reveal my power in you, and so that my name may be proclaimed in all the earth.'[20] Therefore, to whomsoever God wishes God shows mercy, and whomsoever God wishes, he hardens.

So you'll now say to me, 'Then why does God blame [people like Pharaoh]? Who can resist God's will?'

My dear fellow, on the contrary; who are ***you*** to answer back to God? Will what is moulded say to its moulder, 'Why did you make me like this?' Does not the potter have authority over the clay, to create out of one and the same batch one vessel for honourable use and another vessel for less creditable purposes?

And suppose God wanted to show his wrath and to reveal his power, and so with great patience put up with vessels of wrath, ripe for destruction? And [suppose that it was] in order to reveal the riches of his glory, on vessels of mercy which he had prepared beforehand for glory?

All the way through this epistle, Paul has been wrestling (as we must all wrestle) with the mystery of the freedom of God, which can seem dark and harsh at times, but which for Paul is a gracious mercy, one that wants the best for human beings. 'It isn't fair,' the cry regularly goes up from the Society for the Protection of Oppressed Pharaohs – and all we can do is speak of God's gracious freedom! As we worry, however, about the clay that is turned into chamber pots instead of wine goblets (is Paul making a slightly heavy joke here, when he speaks of 'vessels for honourable use . . . vessels for less creditable purposes'?), we need to remember that his attention is far more on the undeserving clay that ends up in the place of honour at a banquet than on its sibling thrust unceremoniously under the bed at night.

Is God's gracious freedom 'fair'?

God concentrates mainly on those whom he has called

24-29 These are the ones whom he called, not only from [among the] Jews, but also from [among the] Gentiles; as he says in Hosea:

'I shall call not-my-people, my-people,
and unloved, beloved.'[21]

---

19. Exodus 33:19
20. Exodus 9:16
21. Hosea 2:23

'And it shall be in the place where it was said to them
"you are not-my-people",
there they shall be called "children-of-the-living-God." '[22]

And Isaiah cries out over Israel:

'If the number of the children of Israel were like the sand of the sea,
the Remnant shall be saved.
For the Lord will act on earth by accomplishing his word, and shortening.'[23]

And as Isaiah predicted:

'Unless the Lord of Sabaoth had left behind offspring for us
we should have become like Sodom
and we should have resembled Gomorrah.'[24]

Again and again we have to allow Paul to force our attention, not on our own plight, nor on that of those (like oppressed Pharaohs) whom we worry about, but on what God's gracious mercy is about. So here Paul is bringing the argument home by way of a string of Old Testament quotations that point to the unexpected mercy of God's action.

Do the Old Testament quotations help you to understand the argument?

Conclusion

30-33 'What then shall we say?' The Gentiles who did not go seeking for righteousness have attained it – but it was the righteousness that came from faith. Whereas Israel, who did go seeking for the law of righteousness, did not even get there. Why? Because they [weren't looking] for the righteousness that comes from faith, but for the righteousness that comes from works. And they stumbled over the stone of stumbling, as it is written:

'Look – I am placing in Sion
a stone for stumbling and a rock for tripping
and the one who believes in it will not be ashamed.'[25]

In conclusion Paul leaves his imaginary opponent with nothing to say. We cannot deserve what God is offering for free, and any attempt to merit it leads to our stubbing our toes (or, to transcribe the Greek rather than translate it, 'being scandalised').

Do you find it difficult to think that we can't possibly deserve what God is offering us?

22. Hosea 1:10
23. Isaiah 10:21, 22
24. Isaiah 1:9
25. Isaiah 28:16

The Law and the Lord

10 [1-13] Brothers and sisters, the desire of my heart, and my prayer for them to God [is] for [their] salvation. For I [can] bear witness that they do [indeed] have zeal for God – but it is not directed by knowledge. For they fail to recognise God's righteousness, and seek [instead] their own righteousness, and have not submitted to the righteousness of God.

You see, Christ is the law's end-and-aim, for reckoning-as-righteous for all who have faith. Moses writes about the righteousness that comes from the law, that 'the one who does them will live by them'.[26] Righteousness that comes by faith, however, says,

'Do not say in your heart
"Who will go up to heaven?"
(That is, bringing Christ down)
or: "Who will go down into the abyss?"[27]
(That is, bringing Christ up from the dead).'

Instead, what does it say?

'The word is near by your mouth and your heart.'[28]
That 'word', of course, is the 'word' of faith that we proclaim.
Because if you confess the Lordship of Jesus with your mouth;
and if you believe with your heart that God has raised him from the dead,
you will be saved.

The point is that it is with the heart that people believe – and that leads to righteousness.

And it is with the mouth that people confess – and that leads to salvation. For Scripture says, 'No one who believes in [him] will be put to shame.'[29]

You see, there is no distinction between Jew and Greek. For they all have the same Lord, who is generous with his wealth to all who call upon him: 'For all who call on the name of the Lord will be saved.'[30]

Paul in this section is still wrestling with the question of his beloved fellow-Jews. Once again he is considering what is wrong with the Law; once again, the answer is that it is not Jesus. Paul surfaces an important idea here, that of the Lordship of Jesus. Remember that calling Jesus 'Lord' (Kyrios, *in Greek) sets him explicitly up against whoever is the Roman Emperor for the time being, and sets him explicitly in relation to God. Read this passage carefully, and see just how close is the relationship that Paul envisages.*

We should also note Paul's clever use of Deuteronomy 30:11-14. In its original context, as Paul and his readers will have known perfectly well, it was

26. Leviticus 18:5
27. Deuteronomy 30:12, 13
28. Deuteronomy 30:14
29. Isaiah 28:16
30. Joel 2:32

about how easy it is to obey the Torah. In Paul's hands, it comes to mean almost the opposite. What matters is not Torah, but Jesus Christ. This underlines the radical novelty of Paul's teaching.

*What is the significance of calling Jesus 'Lord' (*Kyrios*)?*

The position of the Jews

14-21 So how shall they call on the one in whom they have not come to faith? But how shall they come to faith in one of whom they have not heard? And how shall they hear without a proclaimer? And how shall anyone proclaim unless they are sent? (As it is written, 'How beautiful are the feet of those who preach the gospel of good things!')[31]

Ah – but not everyone has obeyed the gospel! For Isaiah says, 'Lord, who believed our report?'[32] So: faith comes from hearing, and hearing is through the word of Christ.

But – I may say – did they not know? Indeed they did: 'Their sound has gone forth to all the earth, their words to the end of the world.'[33]

But – I may say – did Israel [really] not know? In the first place, Moses says,

> 'I shall provoke you to jealousy over what is not a nation,
> over a nation that is foolish I shall provoke you to anger.'[34]

Secondly, Isaiah even has the nerve to say,

> 'I was discovered by those who were not looking for me,
> I became visible to those who were not enquiring after me.'[35]

And to Isaiah he says,

> 'The whole day I held out my hands,
> to a disobedient and obstinate people.'[36]

Paul is still defending God against the charge of lacking integrity for having turned to the Gentiles; and he considers various possible defences ('They never had a chance'), only to dismiss them ('Oh yes, they did'), with a series of scriptural quotations that are probably intended to lay bare the structure of the plight of the Jews:

- *their problem was not that they had not heard the gospel;*
- *their problem was that they had heard and rejected it;*
- *they should have known; they had been warned;*
- *instead, they were 'disobedient' and 'obstinate'.*

But, as we shall see, that is not quite the end of the story.

---

31. Isaiah 52:7
32. Isaiah 53:1
33. Psalm 18:5
34. Deuteronomy 32:21
35. Isaiah 65:1
36. Isaiah 65:2

Has God rejected his people?

11 1-10 My question is then: surely God [cannot have] rejected his people? No way! You see – I am an Israelite, descended from Abraham, of the tribe of Benjamin. God has not rejected his people, whom he foreknew.

Or do you not know what Scripture says about Elijah, how he prays to God against Israel? 'Lord, they have killed your prophets, they have destroyed your altars, and I alone am left – and they are seeking my life.'[37] And how does the oracle respond to him? 'I have left for myself seven thousand men, who have not bent the knee to Baal.'[38]

So therefore, even in the present time, there is a remnant, selected by grace. Now if it is by grace, it is no longer dependent on works, since [in that case] grace [would] no longer be grace.

What is the conclusion, then? What Israel was striving for, it did not attain, but those who were chosen did attain it, and the rest were 'hardened'. As it is written,

'God gave them a spirit of stupor,
eyes not to see, and ears not to hear
until the present day.'[39]

And David says,

'Let their table become a snare to them, and a trap
and a stumbling-block and a retribution to them.
Let their eyes become darkened so as not to see.
Cause their backs to bend for ever.'[40]

We need to watch Paul carefully here; he is heavily involved emotionally, between his love for Christ on the one hand, and his love for his people on the other. The argument has three stages:

1. *I am a loyal Israelite (this is an important 'plank'; Paul wants to eliminate any possible counter-objection that he might be 'against Jews').*
2. *He points to a pattern, found for example in the career of Elijah, a man with whom Paul may have sympathised as sharing his loneliness. It is the people who have rejected God and God's missionaries, not the other way round.*
3. *God always graciously raises up a 'chosen remnant' in Israel, in contrast to those who are (for reasons we do not really understand) 'hardened', perhaps by God himself (like Pharaoh).*

Does Paul's argument 'work' here?

---

37. 1 Kings 19:10, 14
38. 1 Kings 19:18
39. Deuteronomy 29:4; Isaiah 29:10
40. Psalm 69:22, 23

Conclusion (of a sort)

11, 12 'So then, my question is – Surely they didn't stumble so as to fall, did they?'

No way – [what happened was that] because of their fall, salvation came to the Gentiles, in order to make them jealous.

If their transgression enriched the world
and if their defeat enriched the Gentiles,
how much the more [will] their fullness . . . ?

Here the argument seems to reach a term. It may not make much sense to us, unless we recall that all the time, just below the surface of the text, is Paul's conviction of God's unfailing grace (and, of course, his puzzlement that his fellow Jews cannot see what to him is as plain as a pikestaff). The argument goes that Israel got it wrong, so the offer went to the Gentiles, not, however, in order to reject Israel, but so that in the end Israel, and everyone else, would return to God.

How does Paul's conviction of God's unfailing grace help the argument?

Gentiles – wipe that sneer off your face! An illustration from horticulture

13-24 [Now] I'm speaking to you Gentiles. Insofar as I am 'missioned to the Gentiles' I glorify my ministry, to see if I might stimulate my fellow-Jews ['flesh'] to jealousy, and save some of them.

You see, if their rejection [meant] the world's reconciliation, what will their acceptance [mean]? It can only [mean] life out of death.

If the first-fruits are holy, so is the whole lump. If the root is holy, so are the branches. And if some of the branches were broken off, and you, who are a wild olive, were grafted on and you became a partner with the root in the olive's richness, don't go boasting over against the branches – if you do that, [remember] it isn't you that support the root, but the root that supports you.

You may say, 'Branches were cut off, so that I might be grafted on.' OK – they were broken off because of a failure in faith.

And you are in place because of faith. Don't start thinking high-and-mighty thoughts: be in awe! Because if God didn't spare the branches that belong by right to the tree, he won't spare you, either.

So keep an eye on God's generosity – but also God's severity. God is severe on those who fail, but generous to you, ***provided*** that you persevere in his generosity, since you also will be cut off.

As for the Jews, provided they do not continue in their failure in faith, they will be grafted on; for God is well able to graft them on. You see, if you, who were from the wild olive [which is of a different species], have been grafted on to the domestic olive, how much more will those who are of the same species be [able to be] grafted on to an olive of the same species?

Paul now comes at last to the question that he has been circling since that agonised opening to Chapter 9. It seems that he almost drifts into the illustration of the branches of the 'wild olive' grafted on to the root of the 'domestic olive', and we may fear that Paul's grip on the techniques of olive-farming is a bit sketchy; nevertheless, the point is clear enough:

- *it is all about the undeserved generosity of God,*
- *to which we (whether Jew or Gentile) must respond in faith;*
- *it is underpinned (as so often before in this letter) with a 'how much the more' argument.*

Does Paul's argument succeed, do you think?

Conclusion: God's mercy

25-32 You see, brothers and sisters, I want you to understand this secret, so that you should not regard yourselves as clever, because Israel underwent a partial hardening until the full number of Gentiles should come in – and that is how all Israel will be saved, as it is written,

'From Sion the Deliverer shall come forth;
he shall turn away godlessness from Jacob
and my covenant shall be theirs.'[41]
'When I take away their sins.'[42]

As far as the spread of the gospel is concerned, they are enemies [of God], on your account.

However, as far as election is concerned, they are beloved, on account of the ancestors.

You see, God's gracious gifts, and God's calling, are not to be revoked. Just as you, once upon a time, had no faith in God, but now have received mercy because of their failure in faith, so [your Jewish brothers and sisters] failed in faith, and you received mercy, only so that they also should now receive mercy.

For God has imprisoned everyone in failure-in-faith, in order to have mercy on everyone.

We shall not really grasp what Paul is saying, all the way through the letter to the Romans, unless we focus all the time on the inner logic of his argument, which is, quite simply, that God gives his gift out of love for us, not out of admiration for our achievements. It follows that any complacent smirking on our part is a huge misunderstanding, not to say perversion, of God's offer of salvation. We are all on the same footing.

Do you find yourself thinking 'I'm better than those others'? Do you think that Paul would allow that?

41. Isaiah 59:20, 21
42. Isaiah 27:9

Conclusion: triumphant hymn to God's mercy

33-36 O the depth of God's wealth and wisdom and knowledge!
You can't search out his judgements!
You cannot track down his ways!
For 'Whoever knew the mind of the Lord?
or who was his counsellor?'[43]
'Or who ever gave [God] anything on account,
so that they would be repaid?'[44]
For from him
and through him
and to him
is all.
To God be glory for ever. Amen!

The third main section of the epistle now ends with another of Paul's 'purple passages'. Readers should allow themselves to be 'swept up' by the flood of joy here, because it is really this outpouring of love, rather than the impenetrable argumentation, that animates Paul's profoundest insights about what God has done for us in Christ.

CHAPTERS 12-16: FINAL SECTION – 'BITS AND PIECES'

*The argumentation is all behind us now, and Paul spends the remaining five chapters dealing with what, from some angles, looks like a series of practical instructions such as he frequently offers in other epistles – how to live out the gospel. Is he (very diplomatically) referring to difficulties in the Roman Church (or churches)? The reader must decide. Notice the great big '**So**' with which this new section starts, linking the whole story together. In Romans 1-4 he outlined the plight from which God in Christ has delivered humanity; in 5-8 he outlined our grounds for hope; in 9-11 he considered God's hidden plan with particular reference to the painful question 'What about my fellow Jews, then?' Now, finally, he draws out the practical implications for Christian living, probably with special reference to difficulties in the Roman Church that he and his readers knew about, but which we can only dimly reconstruct.*

General exhortation

12 1-3 ***So*** I invite you, brothers and sisters, by the mercies of God, to offer your
bodies as a living, holy sacrifice that is pleasing to God, your rational worship.
And don't conform to this world – instead let yourselves be transformed by renewing
your minds, so as to test what is God's will, that which is good and pleasing and perfect.

43. Isaiah 40:13
44. Job 41:11

For, through the grace that was given me, I tell everyone among you not to think high-and-mighty thoughts, over and above what it is appropriate to think. No – I'm telling you that your thinking should lead to sober thoughts, each of you as God has apportioned [your] measure of faith.

For once, Paul's directness of speech seems to have left him; apart from a reference to 'worship', where he uses Old Testament language, it is hard to be sure what he has in mind here. Perhaps we should hear the sound of tip-toeing on eggshells. It might be that he is building on that splendid passage on which Chapter 11 ended, appealing to his readers to respond to the God whose love and mercy he celebrated there. But their response must be in terms of the new life that Christ offers, not the old life, the sacrifice of dying animals.

Alternatively, if, as some scholars think, Paul only inserted Chapters 9-11 at a later stage, after writing the rest of the letter, then these words go back to the equally splendid passage at the end of Chapter 8.

The image of the Body (borrowed from 1 Corinthians)

4-8 For just as in a single body we have several limbs (or members), but not all the limbs (members) have the same function, so we are one body in Christ, although we are many; and we are individually limbs (or members) of each other. We have different gifts according to the grace that has been given us:

If it is prophecy, let it be proportionate to the faith;
or if it is service, let it be done in service.
If one is a teacher, let them do it in teaching.
If someone is a comforter, let it be done in comforting.
If someone is a contributor, let it be done with single-minded generosity.
If someone gives aid, let them be in earnest.
If someone shows mercy, they should do it cheerfully.

In 1 Corinthians, which was written before Romans, Paul made excellent use, humorous and penetrating, of the image of the 'body', trying to bring healing to a divided Church. Here he seems to make less use of the possibilities of the image, perhaps because the Roman Church is less divided than its Corinthian counterpart or (if what follows later is taken to hint at divisions in Rome) because he is being diplomatic. Notice, though, that, as in 1 Corinthians, he uses the image very adroitly, slipping between 'individual bodies' (12:1) and the Body of Christ, which is made up of those individuals with their bodies.

How does Paul use the image of the 'body' here?

On Christian living

9-21 Your love should not have any 'acting' about it. You should hate evil, clinging to the good, devoted to each other in Christian love, giving each other the lead in mutual respect. Don't be idle [when you should be] serious. Stay 'on the boil' spiritually, serve the Lord. Rejoice in hope; bear up in trouble, be persistent in prayer. Take your share in the needs of the saints; make a thing of hospitality. Bless your persecutors. Bless them, not curse them! Rejoice with those who rejoice, weep with those who weep.

Think along the same lines as each other. Don't think high-and-mighty thoughts – accommodate yourselves to what is lowly. Don't become thinkers in your own esteem. Don't pay back evil for evil. Have a regard for what is honourable in everybody's eyes.

If it is possible on your side, be at peace with everybody. Don't get your revenge, beloved, but leave room for God's wrath, for it is written, 'Mine is the vengeance – it is I who shall repay',[45] says the Lord. On the contrary, 'if your enemy is hungry, feed them. If they are thirsty, give them a drink. For if you do this you will pile coals of fire on their head.'[46] Do not be overcome by evil; instead, overcome evil by good.

In places here one has simply to guess at the grammar, and sometimes also at the meaning; but the gist is clear. Paul paints an agreeable and attractive picture of Christianity at work. Is he implying that the Roman Church was not doing some of the things he mentions here as desirable for Christians; or is it simply a list of generally desirable qualities?

Respect for the powers that be

13 1-7 Let everyone submit to the supreme authorities. For there is no authority except [that which comes] from God; and those which exist, are appointed by God.

It follows that everyone who resists authority is opposed to the ordinance of God; and those who are opposed will receive judgement for themselves. For rulers are not a terror for [those of] good behaviour but for [the] bad. Do you want not to be afraid of authority? Do what is good, and you will have praise from [them]. For the authority is God's servant for you, to bring about the good. If on the other hand you do what is evil, then be afraid. Not for nothing does authority wear a sword – for authority is God's servant, an avenger [who brings God's] wrath on the one who does evil.

It is necessary therefore to submit, not only because of the wrath of God, but also for the sake of conscience. For this reason also [you should] pay taxes; for they are God's ministers who are engaged on this very task. Repay your debts to everybody, tax to the taxman, and excise duty to the excise-man, reverence to those to whom reverence is due, honour to those to whom honour is due.

Readers are taken quite by surprise when they come to this passage, which seems to come out of a clear sky, quite unexpectedly. Worse than that, it was shamefully used by the apartheid régime in South Africa to lecture Church leaders on the importance of obeying the law.

45. Deuteronomy 32:35
46. Proverbs 25:21, 22

What is going on here? Does it mean that Christians can never resist an unjust government? Clearly Christians down the centuries have not reached that conclusion. It may be useful to make the following points to help the reader think through this passage:

1. *This is Christianity's first attempt to work out the relationship of the group of Christians to the secular law. It may be doubted whether Paul would have expressed himself in quite these terms after he encountered the persecution of Nero, a few years later.*
2. *Paul will have seen for himself the advantages that the Roman empire gave to the would-be apostle, not least the possibility of speedy and safe travel, and the relatively secure despatch of letters.*
3. *It is quite possible that Paul knew that there was an issue about paying taxes among the Roman Christians. If the very negative attitude to Roman political authority that we find in the Book of Revelation was one of the strands of opinion in Rome, or if some of the members of that church knew some version of the story of Jesus' response to the question about the census tax (Mark 12:13-17 and parallels) that may have led to a clash with Christians or Jews whose instincts were to preserve the status quo, then Paul may here be attempting to solve a problem at long range.*
4. *There may also be a hidden warning to rulers, such as you often find in the Old Testament (see, for example, 1 Samuel 8:10-18), that they are obliged to exercise their authority appropriately.*

Do you think Christians ought sometimes to speak out against the government?

Fulfilling the law

8-10 Actually, the only debt you should have is to love each other. For anyone who loves [their neighbour] has fulfilled the law. You see, all that stuff about 'You shall not commit adultery, you shall not kill, you shall not steal, you shall not desire',[47] and any of the other commandments, are summed up in this saying: 'You shall love your neighbour as yourself.'[48] Love does not do any evil to the neighbour – therefore love is the fulfilment of the law.

It is almost impossible to imagine that Paul does not have in mind the story of Jesus' strikingly sympathetic dialogue with the scribe, reported at Mark 12:28-34, significantly, perhaps, in the same chapter to which we pointed with regard to the previous passage, about submission to authority.

On staying awake

11-14 And especially since you know what time it is, because it is now time for you to be aroused from sleep; for our salvation is nearer now than when we came to faith.

47. Exodus 20:13, 14
48. Leviticus 19:18

The night is far gone, and the Day has drawn near. Therefore lay aside the works of darkness, and let us put on the weapons that belong to the light. Let us behave decently, as though in broad daylight, not in carousing and drunkenness, not in sexual excesses, not in quarrelling and jealousy.

Instead, put on the Lord Jesus, and it should not be for the flesh that you are taking forethought, to satisfy its appetites.

Two features of Paul's thought come together here. First, his sense that the Day (presumably of Jesus' Second Coming) is not far off. Second, Paul holds that Christians should maintain very high standards of behaviour.

Is Paul making general observations about appropriate Christian behaviour (as perhaps he did in Chapter 12)? Or is he hinting at things that may be amiss in the Roman Church? The reader must decide.

When Christians disagree

14 1-23 When someone is weak in faith, accept them, but not for the purpose of getting into quarrels about ideological positions. One person thinks that he can eat anything; the weak person eats [only] vegetables. The person who [is willing to] eat anything shouldn't disparage the person who doesn't – for God has accepted him. [Likewise] the person who does not eat should not condemn the one who does. Who are you [to] judge a fellow slave? He will stand or fall before his own Lord; in fact he will stand, because the Lord is capable of causing him to stand. One person regards one day as more important than another; another person treats all days as the same – each of them is fully convinced in his own mind. The person who takes account of days does so for the Lord. The one who eats, eats for the Lord – because he gives thanks to God. And the one who does not eat – it is for the Lord that he abstains from eating; and he gives thanks to the Lord.

You see, none of us lives just for ourselves, and none of us dies just for ourselves. If we live, it is for the Lord that we live. If we die, it is for the Lord that we die. So: whether we live or whether we die, we belong to the Lord. This was the purpose for which Christ died and lived, that he might be Lord over both the dead and the living.

But you [over there], who are you to judge your fellow Christian?

And you, why do you disparage your fellow Christian? For we shall all stand before God's tribunal, because it is written,

> 'I live, says the Lord, for to me every knee shall bow
> and every tongue confess to God.'[49]

Therefore each of us shall give an account of ourselves to God.

So – let us not go in for any more judging of each other. Instead, make this your [aim in] judging: not to put an obstacle or a scandal before your fellow Christian. I am certain, I am convinced in the Lord Jesus that nothing is profane of itself; the exception is that when someone regards it as profane, then it is profane for that person.

49. Isaiah 45:23

For if your fellow Christian is grieved because of dietary considerations, you are no longer behaving in a loving manner. ***Don't*** let your diet destroy the one for whom Christ died. Therefore don't allow what you regard as good to be reviled. Because God's kingdom is not food and drink; God's kingdom is righteousness and peace and joy in the Holy Spirit. For the person who serves Christ in this respect is pleasing to God and esteemed among human beings.

To sum up: let us make our goal whatever tends to each other's peace and upbuilding. Don't tear down God's work, just for the sake of food. Everything is pure, but food is evil when a person eats it in such a way as to cause scandal.

It is good neither to eat meat nor to drink wine, or anything else over which your fellow Christian takes offence. As for you, keep to yourself the faith that you have before God. Congratulations to the person who does not reproach himself or herself on a matter which they approve. The person who is in two minds whether to eat will stand condemned, because [what he does] does not spring from faith; and everything that does not spring from faith is sin.

We may (once more) hear the sound of Paul tiptoeing through a minefield. Not all the details of what he is saying are clear to us; but we must assume that they would have been to his readers. Paul distinguishes a weak person from a strong; the latter ignores dietary rules, and may in so doing shock a weak fellow Christian; it also seems that there may have been disagreement over certain 'days', perhaps Sabbath and Jewish feasts. The answer, as always for Paul, goes back to 'the Lord' and what Paul sees as the inevitable consequence of knowing the Lord: absolute respect for fellow Christians. The teaching here echoes his earlier teaching, in Chapter 13, and in 1 Corinthians 12, about the Body of Christ.

Is there an equivalent in the modern Church of the tensions between the 'weak' and the 'strong' in the Roman Church?

It always comes back to Christ

15 1-13 We who are capable have a duty to put up with the weaknesses of those who are less capable and not to please ourselves. Let each of us please our neighbour with the aim of doing good, and building [people] up. You see, Christ did not please himself; instead, as it is written, 'the reproaches of those who reproach you fell on me.'[50] For what was written earlier was written in order to teach us, so that we might have hope through the endurance and comfort of the writings.

May the God who is endurance and comfort grant you the gift to think the same thoughts with each other according to Christ Jesus, in order that with one mouth and with one mind you may glorify the God and Father of Our Lord Jesus Christ.

Therefore accept each other, just as Christ accepted you, to the glory of God. For my position is that Christ became a servant of the circumcision on behalf of God's

50. Psalm 69:9

truth, in order to confirm the promises given to the ancestors, and in order that the Gentiles should [through the (divine) mercy] glorify God, as it is written,

'Because of this I shall acknowledge you among the Gentiles,
and I shall sing praise to your name.'[51]

And again he says,

'Rejoice, Gentiles, with his people.'[52]

And again,

'All Gentiles, praise the Lord,
and let all the people praise him.'[53]

And again Isaiah says,

'There shall be a root of Jesse
and the one who shall arise to rule the Gentiles;
in him the Gentiles shall hope.'[54]

May the God of hope fill you with all joy and peace by your faith, so that you may abound in hope, by the power of the Holy Spirit.

Notice, not for the first time, how for Paul it always comes back to Christ; what he has done, we must also do, and then Christian communities will look as they should. The reference to 'thinking the same thoughts' is also found in Philippians 2, as he introduces the great hymn to Christ, and we may remember that it was in Philippi that Evodia and Syntyche were squabbling, seriously enough for the news to have reached Paul in prison. Notice, too, the coherence of Paul's thought; when he sums up his message, 'accept each other, just as Christ accepted you to the glory of God', we are right back in the main argument of the epistle.

What do you think is the 'main argument of the epistle'?

Paul talks to the Jewish Community in Rome

14-16 My brothers and sisters, I too, for my part am certain about you, that you are full of goodness, replete with all knowledge, well able to give each other admonitions. I have written to you a little bit boldly, just as a reminder to you, because of the grace given to me by God, for me to be a minister of Christ Jesus to the Gentiles, to serve the gospel as a priest. This is in order that the Gentiles' offering should be acceptable, consecrated in the Holy Spirit.

This is not the only time in Romans that Paul uses this liturgical language: see 12:1. Is he trying to snare the attention of his Jewish readers, and win them to his side?

---

51. 2 Samuel 22:50; Psalm 18:49
52. Deuteronomy 32:43
53. Psalm 117:1
54. Isaiah 11:10

Paul's ministry

17-21 Therefore I have matter for boasting in Christ Jesus, in my work for God. For I shall not have the nerve to speak of anything that Christ did not accomplish through me, [to bring] the Gentiles into obedience, in word and deed, by powerful signs and portents, by the power of God's Spirit.

The result is that I have completed [the task of] preaching the gospel from Jerusalem, in a circle as far as Illyricum. I made it my ambition to preach the gospel where Christ had not been named, so that I should not build on anyone's foundation, but, as it is written,

> 'They shall see to whom it has not been announced about him,
> and those who have not heard will understand.'[55]

See how it always comes back to Christ. Remember the opening words of the epistle: 'Paul, a slave of Jesus Christ'. That is the ground and root of all that he is trying to do in this letter, the basis of his mission to the Gentiles, the insistence on what Christ, God, the Spirit have done. That is why he has gone from Jerusalem to what used to be called Yugoslavia, and why he is proposing to travel still further.

What does Paul mean when he calls himself a 'slave of Jesus Christ'?

Why Paul wants to come to Rome

22-33 For this reason I have often been prevented from coming to you. Now, however, since I no longer have opportunity in these regions, and since I have for many years cherished a desire to come to you, so as to journey to Spain; for I am hoping to see you as I pass through, and to be helped on my way by you, as long as I can have some enjoyment of your company first.

My plan at present is to go to Jerusalem, to give [material] support to the saints. For Macedonia and Achaia have decided to offer some solidarity with the poor among the saints who are in Jerusalem. They have decided – and indeed they owed them something. For given that those Gentiles have shared in [Jerusalem's] spiritual gifts, they owe it to them to minister to them with material gifts. So when I have accomplished this, and have 'signed, sealed and delivered' this sum into their hands, I shall return by way of you into Spain. I am certain that when I come to you it will be in the fullness of Christ's blessing.

I implore you, brothers and sisters, through our Lord Jesus Christ, and through the love of the Spirit, to be my allies in the battle, supporting me with your prayers on my behalf to God, that I may be delivered from disobedient unbelievers in Judaea, and that my assistance to Jerusalem may turn out to be acceptable to the saints, so that I may come to you with joy, and, if God wills, have some rest and recreation with you.

The God of peace be with you all. Amen.

---

55. Isaiah 52:15

Paul has already indicated (1:10-15) why he wants to visit the Roman Church. The reasons there were:

1. *to share a spiritual gift with them and strengthen them;*
2. *to get some mutual comfort from each other's faith;*
3. *to bear fruit in Rome, as he had among other Gentiles;*
4. *to preach his gospel in Rome.*

He gives two further reasons here. First, he has done all he can, from Rome to what we used to call Yugoslavia, and he wants to go to Spain, passing through Rome on the way. Second, and we may hazard a guess that this was uppermost in his mind, he wants their prayers and moral support when he takes the collection from 'Macedonia and Achaia' (Philippi and Corinth, perhaps his two favourite churches) to the impoverished Christians in Jerusalem. It is even possible that his collection might be rejected; the intemperate language of Paul's letter to the Galatians (which was, we recall, written before Romans) will have cost him dear in Jerusalem, and it was possible that they might refuse to accept the collection 'from such a tainted source'. There were strong connections between the Jerusalem Christians and those in Rome, and Paul may have wanted the Roman Church to assist him, not only with their prayers, but also with a friendly 'e-mail' to the effect that 'Paul's all right'. Hence the uncharacteristically diplomatic tone of the Letter to the Romans.

The ending sounds almost like a brief farewell; and some have argued that the letter originally ended here; but Paul normally concludes with several personal greetings, which is what Chapter 16 now gives us.

Why do you think Paul wanted to visit Rome?

The commendation of Phoebe

16 1, 2 I recommend Phoebe to you, a fellow Christian of ours, and deacon of the Church of Cenchreae. I ask you to welcome her in the Lord, in a manner appropriate to the saints, and to help in any matter in which she may need your [help]. For she has been of great assistance to many, including myself.

The translators tend to call Phoebe a 'deaconess', but that is not what the Greek says. Now it must be admitted that a 'deacon' has presumably not yet taken on quite the hierarchical sense that it would attain just a little bit later, but Phoebe, unmistakably a woman, is equally unmistakably a figure of some importance for Paul. If Chapter 16 belongs here, it looks as though she may have been the person entrusted with bearing this weightiest of Pauline letters to its intended recipients. Not only that, but she has evidently helped Paul and many other Corinthians. And she is an official of some kind in the church at Cenchreae. Cenchreae was the easternmost port of Corinth, therefore certainly a wealthy suburb in its own right; and Phoebe may well have been influential among the Christians of Corinth also. Paul was not necessarily the 'male chauvinist pig' that his detractors sometimes depict.

An endless (and pointless?) list of greetings

3-16 Greet Prisca and Aquila, my fellow workers in Christ Jesus. They put their necks on the line for me, and I am grateful to them; and not just me, but all the Gentile churches also. And do greet the church at their house.

Greet Epainetus my beloved, the first convert [literally 'first-fruits', another usage of Old Testament cultic language] to Christ in Asia.

Greet Maria, who has laboured hard among you.

Greet Andronicus and Junia, my kinsfolk and fellow prisoners; they are conspicuous apostles, and were Christians before I was.

Greetings to Ampliatus, my beloved in the Lord.

Greetings to Urbanus, my fellow worker in Christ, and Stachys my beloved.

Greetings to Apelles, a respected Christian. Greet those in the house of Aristoboulos.

Greetings to Herodion, my fellow Jew.

Greetings to those in the house of Narcissus who are in the Lord.

Greetings to Tryphaena and Tryphosa, who worked hard in the Lord.

Greetings to beloved Persis – she worked hard in the Lord.

Greetings to Rufus, that outstanding Christian; greetings to his mother (whom I regard as my own mother).

Greetings to Asynkritos, Phlegon, Hermes, Patrobas, Hermas, and all the brothers and sisters with them.

Greetings to Philologus and Julia, Nereus and his sister, and Olympus, and all the saints who are with them.

Greet each other with a holy kiss.

All the churches of Christ send you greetings.

This section is never read in church; and you can see why. The reader may be puzzled why Paul should in this case single out so many people for mention. The reason, I suggest, is quite a simple one: Paul is on something of a diplomatic mission here, and one of his aims at this point is to remind the Christian churches in Rome that they have a good many people known to them who can vouch for him. They might live in Rome, or they might be frequent visitors to the capital. Nor is this at all improbable: Rome was that sort of place, for one thing, 'all roads lead to Rome', and a good many of the empire's inhabitants drifted through, rather to the annoyance of some old-fashioned Romans. For another thing, Paul himself was an inveterate traveller, and all Christians who travelled will have sought out the group of fellow believers in whatever city they reached. So there will have been a good many meetings and conversations, in various parts of the Mediterranean world, on which Paul can build his appeal here.

There are two things for us to notice here. First, the number of women (Prisca, Maria, Junia, Tryphaena, Tryphosa, Persis, Julia, Rufus's mother, Nereus's sister, and any others included in the general list). Second, notice the range of cultures and social classes. Among those with Latin names we have: Prisca, Aquila, Maria (if she is not Miriam, in which case her name would be Hebrew or Aramaic), Junia, Ampliatus, Urbanus, Rufus and Julia. Greek names include several that may well belong to freedmen or slaves: Epainetus, Andronicus, the household of Narcissus, Tryphaena and Tryphosa, Persis, Asynkritos, Phlegon, Hermes, Patrobas, Hermas, Philologus, Nereus, Olympas. And there are names that suggest a Semitic background: Miriam (if she is not Maria), Apelles, the household of Aristoboulos, and Herodion. In addition, we should remember the Jewish practice of having a Hebrew name as well as a name in the local vernacular, so some of the Latin and Greek names may also be given to people of Jewish origin. This is certainly the case for Prisca and Aquila, for example.

Paul may be making a point here about the inclusiveness of God's love. That is what the whole letter has been about, of course.

Why does Paul mention so many names in this letter?

A final plea for unity

17-20 I implore you, brothers and sisters, to watch out for those who cause divisions and offence, contrary to the teaching that you have learnt. Avoid them. For people like this are not slaves of Jesus Christ. Instead they are slaves of their own bellies, and because of their plausible speech and pious language, they [can] deceive the hearts of the unsuspecting.

You see, everyone has heard about your obedience, and so I rejoice over you; but I want you to be wise with regard to the good, but innocent with regard to what is evil.

The God of peace will swiftly crush Satan under your feet.

The grace of Our Lord Jesus be with you.

For Paul, unity was one of the indispensable marks of the Christian churches; and rebuilding unity is in part what this letter has been about. Whatever makes for division, according to Paul, cannot be from the Spirit of God. If we are, like Paul, and, unlike 'those who cause divisions and offence', genuinely 'slaves of Jesus Christ', then our tendency will be to foster unity rather than division. We can guess from Chapter 14 that there have been divisions in Rome, though Paul does not precisely say so, and Paul is determined to help them out of their strife.

What does Paul mean by the phrase 'slave of Jesus Christ'?

Greetings from Christians in Corinth

21-23 Greetings to you from Timothy my co-worker, and from Lucius and Jason, and Sosipater, my fellow-Jews.

Greetings to you from ***me***, Tertius, who am writing this letter in the Lord!

Greetings to you from Gaius, my host, and host of the whole Church here.

Greetings from Erastus, the city treasurer, and Quartus, who is also a Christian.

Once again, Paul insists on passing on greetings; for him this was an important thing to do. Timothy, half-Jewish and a team-mate of Paul's; Lucius, Jason and Sosipater could be Jewish, by the sound of their Greek names. Tertius

(Paul's unfortunate secretary), Quartus (Tertius's brother?), and Gaius (who has a house big enough to contain a huge group of Christians at once), all have Latin names. Erastus has a Greek name, and is evidently an important city official. Incidentally, he could be the 'aedile' (or 'treasurer') named in an inscription on a pavement that was recently discovered in old Corinth.

A mysterious conclusion

25-27 To the One who can strengthen you, according to my gospel and according to the preaching of Jesus Christ, according to the revelation of the mystery that was wrapped in silence for eternal ages, but has at last been made known in the prophetic writings, in accordance with the decree of the eternal God, and has been made known to all the Gentiles for the obedience of faith, to the only wise God, through Jesus Christ, to whom be the glory for ever. Amen.

These closing verses, which are unmistakably from Paul's hand, and clearly fit the main argument of the epistle, are found in various places in the manuscripts: after Chapter 14, or after Chapter 15, or both at the end of Chapter 14 and in their present position. For our purpose that does not really matter, though it may raise questions about whether Chapter 16 was originally a part of the letter.

Notice how Paul begins and ends (as always) with God and Jesus Christ; how he speaks of 'my gospel', which Paul has been defending; how he links his message to the 'prophetic writings', while admitting the divine silence on the matter; notice his phrase 'obedience of faith'; and, finally, the fact that the message is made known to 'all the Gentiles'.

What do you think the Letter to the Romans has been about?

The First Letter to the Corinthians

The First Letter to the Corinthians

If you move from Romans directly to 1 Corinthians, you cannot help but be struck by the difference of tone, far less measured and far more intimate than the previous letter. When Paul wrote to the Romans, he was addressing a community that he had not founded, and who had reason to be suspicious of him. With the Corinthians he had a more intimate relationship, so that the reader will find that he mixes affection and anger to a degree that can seem remarkable until we remember that this is how things happen in families.

The opening address

1 1-3 Paul, called [to be] an apostle of Jesus Christ through the will of God; and Sosthenes [our] fellow Christian, to the Church of God which is in Corinth; to those who have been made holy in Christ Jesus, [who have been] called [to be] saints, along with all those who call upon the name of Our Lord Jesus Christ in every place, both their Lord and ours: grace to you and peace, from God our Father and the Lord Jesus Christ.

In the ancient world, as in the modern world, the opening lines of a letter could very often be a mere formality; but Paul makes the conventions of letter writing work for him. We notice the following points:

- *He is 'called to be an apostle . . . through the will of God'. This is not a job which he has chosen for himself, but one for which he believes he has a divine vocation.*
- *Paul is not alone, but operating in solidarity with other 'fellow-Christians', such as Sosthenes.*
- *Notice his obsession with Jesus, who is mentioned four times in these three verses. It sometimes seems that Paul can hardly write a sentence without mentioning his beloved.*
- *One of the difficulties of Corinth was that the Christians there had something of an obsession with their own spiritual achievements. See how delicately he reminds them 'who have been made holy . . . who have been called to be saints', that like him they are the beneficiaries of God's generous action.*
- *Obsession with our own achievements can blind us to the claims of others. Hence Paul's reference, again rather delicate, to 'all those who call upon the name (i.e. not just in Corinth) and to 'both their Lord and ours' (i.e. Jesus is not their private property).*
- *Note, finally, the end of the address: 'grace and peace' are wished on them, 'from God our Father and the Lord Jesus Christ'. Keep in mind, but do not yet answer this question: what is the relative status for Paul of God and the Lord Jesus Christ?*

It may help you in your reading of the letter to know that (as Paul indicates at 7:1) the Corinthians have written him a (possibly rather self-satisfied) letter, with lots of questions to Paul; we may imagine them wondering, all the way through the first six chapters, when he is going to get round to answering it.

The thanksgiving

4-9 I give thanks to my God all the time about you, because of the grace that has been given to you in Christ Jesus. Because you have been enriched in him in every respect, in every kind of speech, and in every kind of knowledge, just as the testimony of Christ has been confirmed in you. The result is that you are lacking in none [of God's] free gifts, and you are waiting for the revelation of Our Lord Jesus Christ. He will confirm you to the end as blameless in the day of Our Lord Jesus Christ. God is faithful, through whom you were called into the solidarity of his son Jesus Christ Our Lord.

It was conventional in Paul's world to add a thanksgiving to the gods after the opening of a letter; but Paul really makes it work for him – it is no mere formality. Once again, he emphasises that what has happened to the Corinthians is not their achievement. He speaks of 'the grace that has been given to you in Christ Jesus . . . you have been enriched . . . the testimony has been confirmed in you...God's free gifts' (or 'charisms'). He even tells them that 'you are waiting for the revelation of Our Lord Jesus Christ', when perhaps they thought they had already received it, and that any 'blamelessness' of theirs was their own doing.

We should also notice Paul's use of the word that I have translated as 'solidarity'. This is a very important part of his understanding of Christianity. The Greek word is koinonia*, and it means things like 'partnership, union, community, communion, teamwork'. So it is a very rich word – and it points to something that the Corinthians desperately lacked.*

Notice, once again, Paul's obsession with Jesus Christ, and ask, once more, what status he gives him. See in particular how the Old Testament idea of the 'Day of the Lord' has become 'the Day of Our Lord Jesus Christ', and ponder what Paul is saying here.

Confronting division

10-17 I beg you, my fellow Christians, through the name of Our Lord Jesus Christ, that you all say the same thing; and [I beg you] not to have divisions among you, but that you should be made complete in the same mind and the same way of thinking. For it has been revealed to me about you, my fellow Christians, by Chloe's people, that there are squabbles among you; what I mean is that each of you is saying 'I'm for Paul,' or 'I'm for Apollos,' or 'I'm for Kephas.' Well ***I'm*** for Christ!

Is Christ divided? Was it Paul that was crucified for you? Was it in Paul's name that you were baptised? I give thanks to God that I baptised none of you (except Crispus and Gaius), so that no one can say you were baptised in ***my*** name. (And I also baptised the household of Stephanas; but I don't know that I baptised anyone else.)

You see, Christ did not send me to baptise but to preach the good news – not with clever speeches. Otherwise, the Cross of Christ might be emptied [of meaning].

Paul wastes no time in approaching the point. The Christians in Corinth were divided. They were not 'saying the same thing' (compare Philippians 2:2 for a similar appeal, based likewise on Christ and on the gospel). Paul is clearly furious about the divisions, which the Corinthians have presumably not mentioned in their letter to him.

How many parties were there at Corinth? At least three, and perhaps four, each attached to a particular personality. In the translation I have taken it as three (and there is a weight of scholarship on what each of these might have stood for), and the fourth as Paul's grim comment on their divisions: 'as for me, ***I*** *belong to Christ'; but it has to be said that not all scholars would agree.*

Then Paul attacks those who were marching up and down with placards reading 'Viva Paul, viva!' (and presumably he would apply the same analysis to the other parties, but diplomatically avoids the trap). Christ is (as always) the central figure for Paul; Christ (not Paul) was crucified for them, and it was in Christ's name that they were baptised (not Paul's, or Apollos's or Kephas's). This is perhaps why Paul gets into that confusion about whom precisely he had baptised, a confusion that I have tried to convey by the use of parentheses. I imagine him dictating in a room in Stephanas's house in Ephesus, perhaps in Stephanas's presence; he says, 'I baptised none of you', at which Stephanas hisses, 'You baptised Crispus and Gaius'; Paul then makes the necessary correction and proceeds, only to be stopped by another hiss: 'You baptised ***our*** *household!' But you may like to think of other explanations of the text as it stands. He returns, however, to Christ, as always, and to the importance of the Cross, a theme with which he will stay for a while.*

'Is Christ divided?' How would Paul write to the Christians in your city or community today?

The rhetoric of the Cross

18-25 For the rhetoric of the Cross is stupidity to those who are on their way to destruction, whereas to us who are on our way to salvation it is the power of God. For it is written,

'I shall destroy the wisdom of the wise
and the intelligence of the intelligent I shall bring to nothing.'

Where is the clever man? Where is the literate person? Where is the debater of this age? Has not God rendered stupid the world's 'cleverness'? For since – by God's wisdom – the world did not know God through its wisdom, God was pleased to save believers through the stupidity of [our] proclamation. Furthermore, since Jews demand miraculous signs and Greeks go looking for wisdom, we for our part proclaim Christ – Christ crucified! For Jews this is an affront; for Gentiles it is stupidity. However, to those who are called, whether they are Jews or Gentiles, it is Christ, God's power and God's wisdom. Because God's stupidity is wiser than human beings and God's weakness is stronger than human beings.

This is a passage of breathtaking audacity on Paul's part. The word that I have translated 'rhetoric' is 'word', and can also mean 'speech', and even

'reason' or 'rationality'. For Paul, the 'spin doctors' of Corinth had nothing to do with God's message, which is so different from their quest for applause that Paul expresses it in a series of daring paradoxes, between 'cleverness' (or 'wisdom') and 'stupidity', and between 'strength' and 'weakness'. The ultimate paradox, of course, is that of the Cross – the miserable death of a condemned and rebellious slave – which Paul sees as God's key move in the saving of the world. This insight enables Paul even to talk of 'God's stupidity' and 'God's weakness'!

The quotation is from Isaiah 29:19.

What does Paul mean by 'God's stupidity' and 'God's weakness'?

When God called the Corinthians

1[26]–2[5] Think about how you were called, brothers and sisters. Not many of you were 'clever', as people understand it; not many were influential or nobly born. It was the stupid things of the world whom God chose, to shame the 'clever'; it was the weak things of the world whom God chose, to shame the 'strong'; and it was the 'low-born' and the 'despised' of the world whom God chose, the 'non-existent', in order to cancel out the 'existent', so that no human being might boast before God.

But it is [thanks to] him that you exist in Christ Jesus, who became our 'cleverness from God' and 'righteousness' and 'sanctification' and 'redemption', so that as it is written,

'Let the one who boasts, boast in the Lord.'

And so it was that when I came to you, my fellow Christians, I came not with any superior rhetoric or cleverness when I proclaimed God's mystery to you. For I determined that all I would 'know' among you was Jesus Christ – and [Jesus Christ] crucified, at that! And as for myself, it was in weakness and fear and great trembling that I came to you. And my speaking was not a matter of seductive and clever rhetoric; I simply demonstrated the power of the Spirit. My aim was that your faith should not depend on human cleverness, so much as on God's power.

We must imagine a stunned and perhaps indignant silence as these words were read out in whichever house the Corinthian Christians were gathered that Sunday. If they were rather fancying themselves as a cut above the rest they will not have been terribly pleased to hear themselves described as 'stupid things', 'weak things', 'low-born and despised' and 'non-existent'. But we shall get Paul wrong if we think of him here as simply trying to put them in their place. There is, undeniably, a touch of that, but Paul's main aim is to lead the focus of their attention away from themselves and towards God and Jesus.

We notice, once again, Paul's emphasis, in this context, on the crucifixion.

And, finally, the circumstances of his first arrival in Corinth are credibly related in Acts 18. Paul's 'fear and trembling' may have been either because of the kind of place that Corinth was, where only the streetwise survived, or because of failure in Athens, when they had laughed at him on the Areopagus because he had spoken of resurrection.

The quotation about 'the one who boasts' is from Jeremiah 9:23.

Imagine yourself one of the Corinthian Christians, perhaps a bit too pleased with yourself. How does this passage make you feel?

The difference between the human and the divine approaches

6-16 We speak of 'cleverness' among initiates: but not the cleverness of this world nor of the rulers of this world, who are being abolished. Instead we are speaking of the cleverness of God, which is wrapped up in a mystery, [the cleverness] which God marked out beforehand, before the worlds [existed], for our glory. This 'cleverness' [or: wisdom] none of the rulers of this world recognised. For if they had done, they would never have crucified the Lord of Glory. Instead, as it is written,

'What eye has not seen and ear not heard,
and [what] has not come on the human heart,
what God has made ready for those who love him.'

It is to us that God has revealed [it] through the Spirit. For the Spirit searches everything, even the depths of God. For who among humans knows the affairs of the human person, except the spirit of that person which is in them?

Similarly, no one knows the affairs of God except the Spirit of God. We, however, have not received the spirit of the world, but the Spirit that comes from God, so that we may know the free gifts that God has lavished on us, the things that we speak of, not in the learned rhetoric of human cleverness, but in the 'rhetoric' that is taught by the Spirit, interpreting spiritual things to spiritual people. The person who lives merely on the human level does not accept what belongs to the Spirit of God; for they regard it as stupidity, and they can't grasp it, because it is discerned spiritually. But the spiritual person investigates everything spiritually; but the spiritual person herself or himself is not investigated by anybody. For 'Who has known the Lord's mind, so as to instruct him?'

But as for ***us***, we have the mind of Christ!

You will see that it is very difficult to decide between 'cleverness' and 'wisdom' as alternative translations of the Greek word sophia, *because, as Paul uses it here, there is a bit of both. The heart of the matter here is the profound distinction, not to say yawning abyss, between God's way of doing things, and the way of the 'flesh' or 'unreformed humanity'. Paul speaks of the 'natural' or 'unspiritual' person; the Greek word* psychikos *is used rather oddly here, but clearly it is intended to contrast with the 'spiritual' person, who operates in God's way. I have tried to express the contrast by way of the idea of the 'person who lives merely on the human level', but nothing quite captures the sense of the original. The point is that the Corinthians were so flaunting their 'wisdom' that they did not grasp that it was merely 'cleverness' when set against what God was about in Christ.*

The citation 'What eye has not seen . . . ' is from Isaiah 64:3; 'Who has known the Lord's mind . . . ' is from Isaiah 40:13.

'We have the mind of Christ.' What do you think Paul means by this?

Two metaphors for unity: a garden, and a building

3 1-17 My brothers and sisters, it was impossible for me to address you as spiritual beings; [I could only address you] as belonging to the flesh, as 'infants' in Christ. I gave you milk to drink, not solid food, because you weren't up to it. And even now you are not up to it; for you are still belonging to the flesh. Because whenever there is factionalism and squabbling among you, aren't you still belonging to the flesh? [Aren't you still] behaving as human beings?

For example, whenever someone says, 'Well, ***I*** belong to Paul', and someone else says, '***I*** belong to Apollos' – aren't you merely human? So what is 'Apollos'? Or what is 'Paul'? [Merely] servants, through whom you came to faith, in each case according as the Lord granted them. It was I who planted; it was Apollos who irrigated, but it was God who made it grow. The one who planted and the one who irrigated are just the same; each of them will get their own reward, according to their labour.

For [Apollos and I] are just God's collaborators. You are God's garden.

Or [if you like], you are God's building. In accordance with God's grace given to me, like a clever master builder, I laid a foundation, and someone else built on top. Let each one check how they build on top. In fact, no one can put down any foundation other than the existing one, which is Jesus Christ. And if a person builds on top of the foundation, gold, silver, precious stones, timber, hay, or straw, each one's work will become clear. For the Day will show it up; because it is revealed through fire. And the fire will test each person's work, [and reveal] what the quality is. If the work that a person has built on [to the foundation] turns out to be permanent, they'll get their reward; but if a person's work gets burnt up, they'll be punished (but they will be saved, although with a scorching, as it were). Don't you know that you people are the Temple of God, and that the Spirit of God dwells among you?

If someone destroys the Temple of God, God will destroy that person: for God's Temple is holy – and it is you people who are that Temple!

Paul starts by reminding his Corinthians (and, once again, we may envisage a not entirely comfortable silence as this portion of the letter is read out in the house-church) of how immature they were when he first evangelised them. And things do not appear to have progressed, sadly enough, for they are **still** *immature! The evidence is their readiness to divide into factions, principally, it would seem, 'Apollonians' and 'Paulists'. When they do so, they are missing the point, which is that Christ is the foundation, and Christ 'is' the Church.*

To get the message across, Paul uses two metaphors. The first is that of a garden, where Paul and Apollos are only gardeners (although the reader will perhaps reflect that as the planter, Paul may have a certain priority over Apollos!); and what matters is what God does.

The second metaphor will run throughout the letter; it is the idea of a 'building', where Paul (once again quietly claiming priority) laid the foundation, while Apollos (and others) has built the superstructure, in materials of varying quality. Once again, the key point concerns Christ: Christ is the foundation. This leads into a further development of the image, that of the congregation as Temple of God, and now we can see, clearly exposed for the first time, the seriousness with which Paul views any division in the Church, and his horror of those who cause such division. We are not far here from the image of the 'body', which in Chapter 12 Paul is going to use, creatively and with humour, to urge the cause of Christian unity. God is the one who matters.

Why is Paul so horrified by the divisions in Corinth?

Summarising the argument so far

3 18–4 5 Let no one fool himself or herself. If someone thinks they are 'clever' by modern standards, let them become stupid, in order to become [really] clever. For this world's 'cleverness' is stupidity before God. For it is written,

'The one who seizes the clever in their craftiness', and again,

'The Lord knows the reasonings of the "clever" – they lead nowhere.'

So – let no one boast in human beings. For ***everything*** belongs to you: Paul, Apollos, Kephas, the universe, life, death, things present and things to come – ***everything*** belongs to you. And you belong to Christ. And Christ belongs to God.

So a person should account us as servants of Christ, and as stewards of God's mysteries. What people look for in stewards is that they should turn out to be reliable.

It is of absolutely no interest to me that I should be judged by you, or by any human Day [of Reckoning]. I don't even judge myself. For I have nothing on my conscience; but that does not mean that God acquits me – it is the Lord who judges me. So – no premature judgement of anything, until the Lord comes; and he will shed light on the secret places in the darkness, and reveal the thoughts of hearts. So each one will get their praise from God.

Here Paul pulls the argument together; his tone is a bit irritable at this point, which suggests that the criticisms (presumably of the 'Apollonians') have got to him. He is still using the word 'clever' or 'wise' (it is obviously on the table, between him and the Corinthians), still reminding them of the centrality of God, and the relativity of all human factions and all human assessment.

'The one who seizes the clever . . . ' is Job 5:13; the next line is from Psalm 94:11.

'Cleverness' is obviously a problem for Paul. Why?

'Puffed up' – Paul turns to sarcasm

6-13 All this, my fellow Christians, I have applied to myself and Apollos, on your account. I want you to learn from our situation the [meaning of] 'nothing beyond what is written', so that you should not get 'puffed up' on behalf of one [of us] against the other.

For who is distinguishing you? What do you have that you did not receive? And if you received [everything], why boast, as though you had not received it? You are already sated! You are already wealthy! Without any help from us you are already reigning monarchs!

If only you ***were*** already reigning – then we could reign along with you!

You see, I think that God has shown us apostles up as last in the queue, as [gladiators] who are going to die; because we have become a public spectacle, for angels and for human beings. We are fools on Christ's account, whereas you are intelligent in Christ. We are weak, whereas you are strong. You are glorious, whereas we are dishonoured. Right down to this present moment we are both hungry and thirsty; we are poorly clothed, and roughly treated, and of no fixed abode, and we struggle away, working with our own hands. When [they] revile us, we bless [them]; when they persecute us, we put up with it. When they slander us, we are conciliatory. We have become the scum of the universe, and everybody's scrapings, right down to this moment.

For the first time, Paul uses the word that I have translated 'puffed up'. Apart from once in Colossians (2:18), 1 Corinthians is the only New Testament text that employs the word (see 4:6, 18, 19; 5:2; 8:1; 13:4). It is possible that it was a term already 'on the table', between Paul and his Corinthians, and so I have put it into inverted commas. It carries the idea of one of those toads that frightens off its enemies by blowing itself up into a kind of football, and Paul uses it of his opponents, to indicate that they are not 'the real thing'.

So the issue here is not that between Apollos and Paul, but the problem between different Corinthian factions. Paul is very cross, though, as the sarcasm of this passage indicates. We also notice that he hints at the suffering that he has endured for the gospel's sake; and the Corinthians must have known about it, or there would have been no point in Paul's mentioning it. But the sarcasm, and the insistence on his own suffering, also reveals something of the slightly uncertain relationship he had with the Corinthian Christians.

Why does Paul emphasise his own sufferings?

Corinthian factionalism – the final appeal

14-21 [Don't get me wrong] – I'm not writing this to you in order to make you ashamed, but to admonish my beloved children. You may have had ten thousand tutors in Christ – but not all that many fathers. For in Christ Jesus, through the gospel, it is ***I*** who fathered you.

So I'm begging you, sisters and brothers, start behaving like me. That's why I send Timothy (he is my beloved and reliable child in the Lord), for him to remind you of my ways of doing things in Christ Jesus, just as I teach them everywhere, in every church.

Some people got 'puffed up' [thinking that] it was not me that was coming. I shall come to you soon enough (if the Lord wills), and then I shall find out, not the rhetoric of those 'puffed-up' people, but what they can do.

For the kingdom of God is not about rhetoric but about what people can actually do. So it's your choice: do you want me to come to you with a cane, or do you want me to come to you in love, and with a gentle spirit?

Paul is shortly to move on to another issue, so he is bringing this issue of their divisions to an end. The Corinthians may (if Paul was not looking at them when they did so) have raised a quizzical eyebrow at his claim that he was not trying to make them 'ashamed', especially when he concludes with a threat to administer corporal punishment. We should notice, however, the unmistakable affection that Paul feels for those whom he regards as his children.

Nevertheless, they have to get it right, and there is a firm warning (to which he will return later) that they must be respectful to Timothy when he comes; but it is clear that Paul would prefer the relationship to remain affectionate.

'Start behaving like me'. What do you think Paul means?

Incest in the community!

5 1-8 It is actually reported that there is sexual immorality among you; and it is sexual immorality of a sort that [you will] not even [find] among the Gentiles: one [of you] has his father's woman!

You people really are 'puffed up' – shouldn't you rather be in mourning, and have the one who commits the crime removed from your community?

I am physically absent; but in the spirit I am present, and as one who is virtually present, this is my final verdict on the person who has committed this crime:

In the name of Our Lord Jesus
with you gathered as a community, and my spirit being there with you,
with the power of Our Lord Jesus,
a person of this sort is to be handed over to Satan
for the destruction of his flesh
so that his spirit may be saved on the Day of the Lord.

There is nothing pretty about your boasting. Don't you realise that [it only takes] a little leaven to leaven the whole lump of dough? Purge out the old leaven, so that you may be a new dough, just as you have none of the [old] leaven.

You see, our Passover has been sacrificed – it is Christ! So let us celebrate the Passover festival, not with the old leaven, the leaven of evil and wickedness, but with the unleavened bread of sincerity and truth.

Paul's horror here is unmistakable. As a good Jew, he had been brought up to believe in the ancient wisdom that our sexual drive is too important and too powerful to be deployed outside the bond of marriage. Corinth, however, like many another international city (particularly, for some reason, cities with harbours and docks), was notorious for its sexual behaviour, although it is possible that the reputation was overdone. The crime here is that of incest with a stepmother. Paul would have been hardly less alarmed at the effects of the so-called 'sexual revolution' of the 1960s; and it is an open question whether the change in patterns of sexual behaviour in the years since that time has increased or diminished the sum of human happiness.

The reference to the Passover may plausibly be taken as an indication of the time of year when the letter was written. In 16:8 he announces his intention of remaining in Ephesus until Pentecost, so it is quite possible that he was writing at Easter time.

Do you think Paul might have had something similar to say to Christians where you live today?

Relations with the sexually liberated outside the community – a clarification

9-13 In [my] letter, I wrote that [you were] not to consort with the sexually immoral. [I did] ***not*** [mean] those 'in the world' who are sexually immoral, or [for that matter] the covetous, and those who are swindlers, or idolaters; because in that case you would have to leave the world entirely! I am now writing to you not to have anything to do with a so-called fellow Christian who is sexually immoral or covetous or idolatrous, or a reviler or a drunkard or a swindler: [you should] not even eat with a person of that sort.

I have no interest in judging outsiders! Isn't it you people [in any case] who will judge insiders? Outsiders will be judged by God. 'Take the evil one from your midst.'

Paul's horror of sexual immorality has led the Corinthian Christians to a confusion that is perhaps pardonable. They thought that he meant eschewing contact with anyone at all who was that way inclined; but that is not his problem. As he half jokingly indicates, if you were to adopt that policy, you wouldn't have a great many people to talk to in contemporary Corinth. His problem is with having people of that sort inside the community, because they contaminate the rest. Here it may be helpful to think of his image of the old and new leaven. And we are verging here on the doctrine that we shall encounter later, of the Church as Body of Christ: if it is Body of Christ, then certain activities may not go on within it.

It may be worth noting that 'take the evil one from your midst' is a quotation from Deuteronomy (13:16; 17:7, 12; 21:21; 22:21), where it refers to the capital punishment of false prophets, idolaters, those who disobey the legal decision of parents, disobedient sons, and girls who are not virgins on their wedding night. Clearly that is not what Paul has in mind here.

Is there a problem here for Christian living in our contemporary world?

A further complaint: litigation in the community!

6 1-11 [Is it true that] one of you has the audacity, when he has a case against another, to seek judgement from the unjust, and not from fellow Christians? Don't you realise that it is Christians who will judge the world? And if it is among you that the world is judged, are you incompetent to judge small claims? Don't you realise that we shall be judging ***angels***, never mind mundane matters? So – if you have competence over mundane matters, [why] are you appointing those of no importance in the Church as judges over you?

Now I [really] am speaking to make you ashamed. So is no one among you clever enough to judge a fellow Christian's case? Instead, are Christians going to law against each other? And before unbelievers?

wife and on marriage as a partnership. The final sentence seems to imply that Paul is a celibate, or at least widowed (which makes life difficult for those who locate a 'Mrs Paul' in Philippi – see Philippians 4:3; unless he is one of those able to remain celibate within marriage).

Do you think that Christians are against sex?

On marital status

8-11 My message to the unmarried and widows is this: it is good for them to stay as I am. If, however, they are not [managing to] control themselves, then let them marry – for it is better to marry than to burn.

To those who are married, my advice (not mine but the Lord's) is that a wife should not separate from her husband; but if she does separate, she should remain unmarried or be reconciled to her husband. And I advise a husband not to abandon his wife.

The context of this passage, we shall see later, is Paul's sense that the end is coming soon, so placing him and his Corinthians in a situation quite different from our own. He remains, too, passionately opposed to any kind of sexual immorality – it does not fit with the Body of Christ.

What does he mean by 'burn'? Scholars are divided between burning passions, and burning in Hell, or in the fire of judgement. You must make your own decision.

Paul does not countenance separation under these circumstances, and certainly not in order to marry someone else!

What if you're married to a non-Christian?

12-16 As for the others (this is me talking, not the Lord): if a Christian man has a wife who is a non-believer, and she is happy to live with him, he should not divorce her. And if a [Christian] woman has a husband who is a non-believer, she should not divorce her husband.

You see, the non-believing husband [can] be sanctified by his [Christian] wife; and the non-believing wife through her Christian [husband]. Otherwise your children [would be] unclean; but as it is they are holy. But if the non-believer [opts for] separation, let them separate; under circumstances like these, the Christian husband or wife is not enslaved: God has called you [to be] in peace. How do you know, wife, but that you'll save your husband? Or, husband, if you'll save your wife?

This is an admirably balanced judgement. Paul is quite realistic about the strains of 'mixed marriages', but also knows of their possibilities.

A general rule in this part of the letter is that Paul is trying to think his way through a new problem, so it represents something closer to a beginning than an end of the Church's positioning with regard to marriage and divorce. And because Paul thought that the present dispensation might not last much longer (perhaps Jesus' Second Coming would be next Wednesday at the latest) he is, as we have said, in a rather different position from ourselves.

Do you think that it might make a difference to your morals if you thought that the Second Coming might be 'any day now'?

What about circumcision and slavery?

17-24 Anyway, as the Lord has given each one their [allotted] portion, as God has called each of them, let them walk in that way. This is the rule I make in all the churches. If someone was circumcised when they were called, let them not undergo the operation to remove the circumcision. If they are called as uncircumcised, let them not be circumcised. Circumcision and uncircumcision are wholly unimportant; [what matters] is the keeping of the commands of God. Everyone should remain in the calling to which they were originally called. If you were called as a slave, don't worry about it. Even if you are able to get free, rather make use of your situation. For the one who is called in the Lord as a slave is the Lord's freedman. Similarly, the one who was free when called is Christ's slave.

You were purchased at a price – don't get enslaved to human beings. [So], brothers and sisters, as each of you was called, so you should remain before God.

Obviously the Corinthians have asked whether turning to Christ meant an end to social and ethnic and religious distinctions such as slavery and circumcision. Paul wants them instead to concentrate on what God has done for them in Christ (although he is clear that these conventional distinctions are irrelevant within Christianity). So they are not to bother about changing status, including the status of slavery, interestingly enough, although here Paul's Greek is so skeletal that it could mean either 'make use of your status as slave' or 'make use of your opportunity to be free'.

Once again, notice how the word 'Lord' is used: is it God, or Christ, and what difference does Paul make between them?

'Circumcision' and 'Slavery' were burning issues in Paul's world, in a sense in which they are not today. What are the modern equivalents, posing awkward questions for the Church?

What about virgins?

25-38 About the unmarried, I have no command of the Lord; instead, I am giving my opinion as one whom God's mercy has enabled to be faithful. So – I think the following is appropriate, because of the constraints of the present time; it is good for a person to be as they are. If you are bound to a wife, don't seek for a dissolution; if you are free, don't look for a wife. But you don't sin if you get married; and if the unmarried woman gets married, she does not sin. [The only thing is] people like that have trouble in the flesh, and I'm [trying to] spare you that.

This is what I mean, my fellow Christians: the time is contracted. For what remains, let those who have wives be as though they had none; and those who weep, as though they were not weeping, and those who rejoice as though they were not rejoicing and those who are in commerce as though they had nothing, and those who have dealings with the world [must be] as though they were not dealing completely with it. For the outward form of this world is passing away.

I want you to have no worries. The unmarried person is worried about the Lord's affairs – how are they going to please the Lord? Whereas the person who gets married is worried about the world's affairs – how is he going to please his wife? And he is divided.

Likewise, the unmarried woman who is not in marriage, and the virgin, are concerned about the Lord's affairs – to be holy in body and in soul. Whereas the woman who gets married is concerned about the world's affairs – how can she please her husband? I'm saying this to help you, not to put a halter on you. [It's just that] I want everything to be [done] properly and with constancy to the Lord, without distraction.

If, however, someone thinks they are behaving badly towards their young woman, if it's going too far and it is appropriate that it happens in this way, they're not sinning: let them get married. But anyone who remains steadfast in their heart, and is not under strain, but is exercising mastery over their own will, and has decided on this in their own heart, to keep her as a virgin – he will be doing all right. So: the one who marries his young woman does well, and the one who does not marry will do even better.

We have to read this passage with some care, mainly because it speaks to us from a world that at first sight seems utterly different from our own. We shall do well, however, to remember that with Corinth's reputation for sexual misbehaviour, Paul may well have seen a 'sign-value' in people deliberately remaining unmarried. In addition, of course, we must pick up his references to the 'time' and the sense that everything was coming to an end: remaining unmarried might be difficult, but it would perhaps not be for very long, is the underlying argument. We shall misread the apostle if we see him as a miserable old Puritan, thundering 'Sex is bad, sex is dirty' from his office in Ephesus.

What are the dangers involved in marriage, according to Paul?

What about marriage after bereavement?

39-40 A wife is bound for as long as her husband is alive; but if the husband dies, she is free to marry whomever she wants, but only in the Lord. She'll be happier, however, if she remains as she is, in my opinion.

And I also think I have the Spirit of God!

Paul is making a similar point here (and we may care to notice that this argument appears again, in slightly different disguise, in Romans 7); but observe that he is quite balanced about it. The impression one gets is that his opponents were claiming possession of the Spirit and decrying marriage: 'Asceticism: good; sex: bad', might have been their slogan. Paul's view is that both are good, according to the gifts of God.

'I also think I have the Spirit of God.' What is the claim that Paul is making here?

What about food offered to idols?

8 [1-13] *Now Paul proceeds to answer another of the Corinthians' questions: are they allowed to eat food that has been sacrificed in pagan ceremonies? The advantage would be that the meat would be sold off cheap in the market; the disadvantage would be the impression given that Christians who ate such food were in fact participating in pagan ceremonies.*

As for food offered to pagan deities, we realise that all of us have 'knowledge'. Knowledge 'puffs up' – but love ***builds*** up. If someone thinks that they've got 'knowledge', they don't yet have this 'knowledge' as they ought to know it. On the other hand, a person who loves God is known by God.

As regards eating what has been sacrificed to idols: we know that 'idols have no existence in the world' [Isaiah 41:24] and 'there is only one God' [Deuteronomy 6:4].

For there are so-called 'gods' in heaven and on earth, just as there are many 'gods' and many 'lords'. BUT:

We have one God (the Father),
from whom everything comes – and we [are made] for him.
And we have one Lord, Jesus Christ,
through whom is everything – and we are through him.

But not ***everyone*** has this 'knowledge'. Some people, through force of habit, eat meat as an offering to the pagan deity; and their conscience, because it is diseased, is defiled. Food will not bring us before God'[s judgement-seat]. It is neither the case that if we refrain from eating we go hungry nor that if we eat we have a surplus. But just make sure that this freedom of yours doesn't become a cause of stumbling to those who are [still] sick. You see, if someone sees you (you who have 'knowledge') reclining at dinner in a pagan temple, won't their conscience (because they are still sick) get built up so as to eat food offered to idols? So your 'knowledge' is the cause of the destruction of this person who is sick, a fellow Christian for whom Christ died. So those of you who sin against your fellow Christians and batter their sick consciences, are sinning against Christ.

Therefore, if food is [going to] scandalise a fellow Christian of mine, I'll never, ever eat meat – so as not to scandalise a fellow Christian.

Eating food offered to idols, and thereby running the risk of making people think that we have changed religion, or take pagan deities seriously, is not really a problem for us, as it was in Corinth. In that city, a) you could get meat on the cheap if it had previously been offered in sacrifice (that's how the priests made their money); and b) you might walk past a temple and see someone you knew sharing in a banquet, and either be shocked because they have become a worshipper of Asclepius or Aphrodite, or decide, 'well, in that case I can be a Christian **and** *worship the Roman or Greek gods.'*

What matters to us is the principle Paul uses to solve the problem; the pagan deities are non-existent and therefore unimportant. The focus for us is God and Christ, not the 'knowledge' to which the squabbling Christians were laying enthusiastic claim. It is not knowledge that counts, but love; once again, Paul reverts to the term 'puffed up'; once again, by contrast, he adverts to the image of 'building up'. If you are to be a Christian, it is not theological or technical expertise that counts, but your loving concern for the well-being of the other.

One passage to think about is verse 6, Chapter 8: 'We have one God . . .' Here Paul is deliberately echoing the great Jewish prayer of the Shema ('Hear, O Israel, the Lord your God is One God . . .' – Deuteronomy 6:4; compare Malachi 2:10), asserting monotheism against the polytheism of 'the nations'; and here Paul has cleverly demonstrated how he can assert his native monotheism, and **at the same time** *give Christ the very lofty title of Lord. He does this by way of deft contrast with the pagan world and its many 'gods' and many 'lords', this last a clear side-swipe against the increasing tendency of Rome to insist on emperor-worship. There is a good deal going on in this passage.*

What would be the equivalent for Christians today of 'eating food offered to idols'?

Paul's freedom

9 1-27 *As we read this section, it is important for us to see that Paul is still dealing with the same question: Christians are free, as he has already told the Corinthians, and as they are now quoting back at him. But Christian freedom does not mean that we can do what we like – we are restrained by the Law of God, and by consideration for others. To illustrate this principle, and still with his mind on the question of food offered to idols, and the deeper issue underlying it, of 'liberty or licence', Paul speaks of an issue in his own life which (it seems) his opponents have used against him, the fact that though he is a preacher and therefore entitled to material support, he has, as it happens, paid his way (as a tent-maker, according to Acts 18:3); and although he would have been entitled to have his wife with him, he has not done so.*

What about me? Aren't I free? Aren't I an apostle? Haven't I seen Jesus Christ our Lord? Aren't you my work in the Lord?

If I'm not an apostle to others, I am at least an apostle as far as you are concerned – for you are the certificate of my apostolic mission in the Lord. This is how I defend myself against the people who are putting me on trial.

Clearly we have the right to food and drink. Clearly we have the right to take a Christian wife around with us, like the other apostles, and the Lord's brothers, and Kephas. Or is it only I and Barnabas who do not have the freedom not to work? Whoever fought in a campaign at their own expense? Who plants a vineyard and doesn't eat of its fruit? Who shepherds a flock and is not fed on the flock's milk?

Am I just arguing from a human point of view – doesn't the Law say this? For in the Torah of Moses it is written, 'You shall not muzzle an ox that is treading the grain.' Do you think God is worried about oxen? Or is he not certainly talking about us? It was on our account that it was written that the ploughman ought to plough in hope, and the thresher in hope of having his share. If we have sowed spiritual seed among you, is it a very big deal if we harvest your material crops? If [certain] other people have a share in your freedom, should we not, even more so?

Instead, [however] we have not made use of our freedom, but are silent about everything, so as not to throw a spanner in the works of Christ's gospel.

Don't you realise that those who perform the sacred rites eat from what the temple affords? Those who serve at the altar share in its profits. So the Lord laid it down for those who proclaim the gospel to live off the gospel.

Now I have made use of none of this; and I am not writing all of this so that this should happen in my case. You see, I'd rather die than – no one will invalidate my reason for boasting. If I preach the gospel, that's no grounds for me to boast. For it's something I ***have*** to do: I'm in ***pain*** if I don't preach the gospel. If I do this voluntarily, I get my salary; if I do it reluctantly, I'm entrusted with a commission. So what's my salary? It is [simply] to offer the gospel free of charge, so as not to abuse my freedom in the gospel.

I'm free of anybody's claims; and yet I've enslaved myself to everybody, in order to gain more people. And [so] to the Jews I was like a Jew, in order to win over Jews, under the Torah to those under the Torah, even though I wasn't myself under the Torah, in order to win over those under the Torah. To those outside Torah, I became like one outside the Torah; it wasn't that I was outside God's Torah, for I was within Christ's Torah, in order to win over those not under Torah. To the weak I became weak, in order to win over the weak. To everybody I became everything, in order in every way to save some of them. I do everything for the gospel's sake, in order that I may have some partnership in it.

[Think of the Isthmian Games]: you're surely aware that the people who are running in the stadium, all of them run, but only one gets the gold medal. Run in such a way as to win it. Everyone who is in training is under all kinds of discipline. Now they do it to win a glory that passes; but our training is for a glory that never passes. So my running is done with a clear end in view; and when I box, I make sure that my punches don't miss their target. Instead, I treat my body roughly, and make it my slave, because my fear is that having preached to others, I myself might not pass the test.

This chapter starts with an angry series of rhetorical questions (and when you meet Paul, you will do well to answer all of them with a solid affirmative; his temper is just a shade uncertain), and ends with an athletics metaphor. We speak nowadays of 'inculturation', which (among many other things) can mean preaching the gospel in terms that the host culture can understand. The Corinthians lived only a few miles from the site of the biennial Isthmian Games, and may have appreciated the metaphor Paul uses, while perhaps reflecting that (as a good Jew) he was not perhaps entirely at home in the world of the locker room.

In between the angry questions and the attempt to win their interest by a familiar allusion, Paul pursues his central argument, that in order to make sure that the gospel is properly preached, he has foregone his rights. The Corinthians, if they are listening carefully, should be reflecting on how this applies to their question about eating the meat that has been sacrificed in the temples of their city.

Two other points: first, the word he uses early in the fifth paragraph, which I have translated 'we are silent about . . .' can also mean 'we bear everything'. It is not a particularly common word, and it appears again in 1 Corinthians 13. Perhaps Paul's mind is running ahead of itself already to that beautiful hymn, which is his third answer to all their divisions, the 'hymn to love'.

Second, notice the broken syntax, probably expressing his deep emotion, two paragraphs later: 'You see, I'd rather die than – no one will invalidate my reason for boasting'. We shall not understand Paul unless we realise how much the preaching of the gospel means to him.

Why does preaching the gospel mean so much to Paul?

Appeal to biblical precedent: how to read the Old Testament

10 1-13 My fellow Christians, I want you to be absolutely clear that our ancestors were all under the cloud, and all of them went through the sea. They were all baptised into Moses in the cloud and in the sea. They all ate the same spiritual food and all drank the same spiritual drink. For they drank from the spiritual Rock that followed them – and the Rock was Christ. But God was not pleased with most of them – for they were slain all over the desert. These things happened as 'types' for us, to discourage us from desiring evil, just as they did. And don't be idolatrous, as some of them were, as it is written,

'The people sat down to eat and drink and rose up to play.'

And let us avoid sexual immorality, as some of them committed sexual immorality, and three thousand of them fell in a single day.

And let us not put Christ to the test, as some of them tested him, and they were destroyed by snakes.

And don't complain, as some of them complained, and were destroyed by the Destroyer.

These things [as I say] happened to them as a 'type'; but they were written down to admonish us, on whom the ends of the ages have arrived.

So let everyone who thinks that they are secure watch out for a fall. The only temptation that has seized you is of a human kind. God is faithful; and God will not permit you to be tempted beyond what you can manage. Along with the temptation, he will fashion a successful outcome, so that you['ll] be able to bear up under it.

Paul is still trying to deal with the question of eating food that has been sacrificed to idols, while not surrendering his belief in the freedom of Christians. Unless you keep your eye on the ball, however, you may not see quite where he is going.

He appeals to the Exodus story in the Old Testament, especially recalling by his quotation of Exodus 32:6 that terrible memory of the episode of the

Golden Calf. This may perhaps indicate that it was Corinthian **Jewish** *Christians who were most anxious about this issue; but because for him Christ is God's last word, he feels entitled to reread the Old Testament story from a Christian point of view. So he speaks of the desert ancestors as 'baptised into Moses', and (without having to argue for it) of the 'Rock' (from which they drank) as Christ. The worst thing they did in all that time was to worship the Golden Calf (see Exodus 32); but (like some Corinthians) they also committed sexual immorality, and complained about their leaders. No one can think themselves immune. So even if they think they are strong, it may be better to forgo their right.*

Should Christians always be prepared to forgo their rights?

Summarising the debate

10[14–]11[1] Therefore, my beloved ones, avoid idolatry. I am speaking to prudent people: judge for yourselves what it is that I am saying. The cup of blessing which we bless – is it not an act of communion with the blood of Christ? The bread which we break – is it not an act of communion with the body of Christ?

Because there is one loaf, we who are many are one body; for we all partake of the one loaf.

Look at Israel according to their physical ancestry: those who eat the sacrifices are in communion with the altar of sacrifice.

What is my point? That stuff sacrificed to idols, or an idol itself, is of any importance? No – what I am saying is that their sacrifices are sacrificed to demons, and not to God; and I don't want you to end up in communion with demons. It is just not possible to drink both the Lord's cup, and the cup of demons. It is just not possible for you to share the Lord's table and the table of demons. Or are we provoking the Lord to jealousy? We're not stronger than him, are we?

Yes, 'freedom in everything'; but not everything is profitable.

'Freedom in everything'; but not everything builds up [the body]. No one should be looking for their own interests, but for the interests of the other person.

Eat anything that is bought in the market; and don't ask too many awkward questions, because of [your] conscience. 'The Lord's is the earth, and the fullness thereof' [Psalm 24:1]. If a non-Christian invites you to a meal, and if you are minded to go, eat everything that is put before you, asking no awkward questions, because of [your] conscience. If, however, someone tells you 'this was sacrificed in a temple', don't eat it, because of the person who pointed it out to you, and for the sake of conscience. When I say 'conscience', I don't mean yours, but theirs. For why should my freedom come under judgement from someone else's conscience? If I have a share in grace, why am I slandered because of what I give thanks for?

To sum up: whether you eat or drink, or whatever you do, do everything for the glory of God. Don't give offence to [anyone]: Jews, Greeks, the Church of God, just as in every way I please everybody, not seeking my own advantage, but the advantage of the greater number. [I want] them to be saved. Be imitators of me, just as I am [an imitator] of Christ.

Paul brings this complex and difficult argument together with splendid simplicity; but he takes the opportunity to cast the net wider than just the question of food offered to idols. Obviously idolatry is out; but deeper than that is the unity of the Christian group, symbolised and made actual by the bread and wine of communion. Once again the idea of 'Body of Christ' comes to the surface; here it has two meanings, the 'eucharistic body' and the 'body of Christians', and Paul makes intelligent use of the ambiguity.

Once again he touches on the word koinonia *(union, communion, solidarity, etc.), and emphasises that we have to choose: Christ or demons? So our Christian 'freedom' is not to be asserted without further ado: our obligation is not to ourselves, but to look out for the interests of our fellow-members of the body.*

Finally, but only after this necessary preliminary has been carefully laid out (remember that it was in all probability the first time that the Church had had to face this particular question), Paul makes a sensible practical suggestion: it's all right to eat this food, but not if someone makes a thing of it. Notice that the last word in the section is 'Christ'. It is in for ever coming back to Christ that Paul solves all his problems.

What are the limits on Christian freedom?

Styles of headdress in worship

Perhaps we need to know more about life in Corinth in Paul's day, to understand these lines

2-16 I applaud you [when you tell me] that you remember me in every way, and that you hold fast to the traditions, just as I passed them on to you.

I want you to be clear that of every man, Christ is the head; and the man is the head of his wife; and Christ's head is God.

Any man who has anything on his head when praying or prophesying brings shame on his head. Whereas any woman who has her head uncovered when she prays or prophesies brings shame on her head – for it's exactly the same as a woman who has been shaved. For if a woman doesn't wear a covering, let her have it cut short. But if it is disgraceful for a woman to have it cut short or shaved – let her wear a covering.

You see, a man ought not to have his head covered, because he is the 'image and glory of God' [Genesis 1:26]. Whereas the woman is the 'glory of the man': for the man did not come from the woman, but the woman from the man. And then the man was not created on the woman's account, but the woman on the man's account. This is the reason why the woman ought to have control over her head, on account of the angels.

But, of course, in the Lord there is no such thing as woman without a man or man without a woman. For just as the woman is from the man, so the man is through the woman: and it all comes from God.

Judge for yourselves: is it decent for a woman to pray to God with her head uncovered? Doesn't nature teach you that if a man has long hair it is his disgrace, while if a woman has long hair it is her glory? Because long hair is given her as a covering.

And if anyone wants to pick a fight, we have no such custom, and neither do the churches of God.

In our day we approach this passage with some trepidation, because we are shy of anything that would seem to argue that women are inferior to men, and therefore nervous even of stressing (as Paul does here) the difference between women and men. In reading this passage, the following observations may be helpful:

- *Paul is displaying much emotion here, so it is obviously a matter of considerable importance to him.*
- *He may, however, be aware that his arguments will not, perhaps, convince all of his Corinthian audience. So he argues from creation (the chain that goes God-Christ-man-woman), from liturgical propriety ('because of the angels'), from natural law (short hair for men, long hair for women), and, finally, perhaps feeling that he needs a coup de grâce, from authority ('we have no such custom, and neither do the churches of God').*
- *The words for man and woman also mean husband and wife in Greek, and we need to read this into the passage.*
- *Paul is definitely not arguing the inferiority of women: they are allowed the same liturgical function as men (praying and prophesying), and he is adamant about their mutual independence in the Lord. So he will not surrender his 'gospel of freedom', whatever is the issue in Corinth (and many scholars suggest that the problem may have been men dressing as women and women dressing as men).*
- *The force of the arguments (e.g. 'because of the angels') is now lost to us, and we have to assume that they meant more to Paul and his Corinthians. Scholars have spilt much ink on them, but the jury is still out.*
- *Part at least of the argument depends on two different meanings of 'head': that which you find at the top of the body, and 'authority'.*
- *Paul starts by applauding the Corinthians for observing his traditions. Now he goes on to criticise their failure to observe an important tradition that he gave them.*

What would be the equivalent of this issue today?

Divisions at the Eucharist!

17-34 In giving you this direction, I am not [able to] applaud you on another matter. When you gather as a community, you do more harm than good.

For in the first place, when you gather as a church, I hear that there are splits among you, and I partly believe it. For it's inevitable that there should be dissensions among you, so that the tried and true among you may be revealed.

So: when you gather in the same place as a community, it is not for eating the Lord's Supper. For each of you wolfs down your own supper ahead [of the others]: and this person goes hungry, while that person is drunk! Don't you have homes for eating and drinking in? Do you have contempt for God's Church? Do you embarrass the 'have-nots'? What can I say to you? Shall I applaud you? On this matter I cannot applaud you.

For ***I*** received from the Lord, what I also passed on to you, that the Lord Jesus, on the night when he was handed over, took bread, and, giving thanks, broke it and said, 'This is my body, which is for you: do this in memory of me.'

Likewise, the cup, after supper: 'This cup is the new covenant in my blood. Do this, as often as you drink it, in memory of me.'

For as often as you eat this bread and drink this cup, you proclaim the Lord's death until he comes.

So – whoever eats the Lord's bread or drinks the Lord's cup unworthily is guilty of the Lord's body and blood. Let a person examine themselves, and in that frame of mind eat of the bread and drink of the cup. For the one who eats and drinks, eats and drinks condemnation for themselves if they do not discern the body.

This is the reason that many people among you are sick and ill – and quite a few have died. If we have an accurate discernment of ourselves, we shouldn't get condemned. But if we are condemned by the Lord we are punished, in order not to share in the world's condemnation.

So, my brothers and sisters, when you come together for the meal, show hospitality to each other. If one of you is ravenous, have a meal at home, so that your community gathering may not be a source of condemnation. The other matters I shall put in order when I come.

The opening of this section tells us that the reports about divisions were not included in their letter; the end of it apparently dismisses 'the other matters' in their letter as of no urgency.

Central, however, to Paul's understanding of what it is to be a Christian community, is the question of unity, especially at the Eucharist. Paul is horrified to hear of the class distinctions operative at the Corinthians' communion service: some are drunk, and others are starving! As always with Paul, the solution goes back to Jesus, and, in this case, to what he did 'on the night when he was handed over'. It goes back to the extraordinarily weighty significance that Paul (and Christians before and since his time) attached to Jesus' mysterious words and gestures at the Last Supper, 'This is my body . . . This cup is the new covenant in my blood'. Whatever the precise meaning of this formula, it is not something to be treated lightly.

Paul here once more makes good use of the idea of 'body', which has resonances of both the 'community of Christians' and the 'eucharistic body of Christ' (and there is probably also a hint of the body of Jesus that suffered on the Cross, in what he says here).

We should notice also Paul's reference to the fact that 'quite a few have died', looking ahead to an issue that he will have to confront in Chapter 15.

What is the nature of the divisions at the Eucharist in Corinth? How might they appear today?

WHAT ABOUT THE CHARISMATIC GIFTS? (12:1–14:40)

One of many sources of division in the Corinthian community was evidently the distribution of 'spiritual gifts', and my easy assumption that I'm a better Christian than you because I speak in tongues, or prophesy, or work miracles, or whatever, and you don't. Paul spends quite a long time now (three chapters in our division of the letter), trying to work out the principles on which to resolve this one.

A simple test

12 1-3 As regards spiritual gifts, my fellow Christians, I don't want you ignorant.
You know that when you were pagans, you would get led astray, taken off to dumb idols. So I'm telling you: no one who is speaking with the Spirit of God can say 'Jesus is cursed.' Likewise, no one can say 'Jesus is Lord,' except by the Holy Spirit.

As always, Paul brings it back to Jesus, and a simple test: what is the charismatic's attitude to Jesus? If they (charismatics) proclaim Jesus as 'Lord' as Paul does, again and again, then they are led by the Spirit. Could one imagine anyone uttering the opposite statement, that 'Jesus is anathema?' One possibility is in time of persecution, when perhaps Christians were invited to say this, and to proclaim that 'the Emperor is Lord', to avoid torture or a horrid death, although it is not clear that, by the time 1 Corinthians was written, the Church had met with the persecution that would soon afterwards start to be the inevitable concomitant of the proclamation of the gospel. Perhaps also this odd-sounding statement is a rule of thumb whereby to assess the utterances of charismatics in the Church.

What is **your** *attitude to Jesus?*

Diversity and unity in the Church

4-11 There are different kinds of spiritual gifts, but the same Spirit.

There are different kinds of service, and the same Lord.

There are different kinds of activities, but the same God who enacts everything in everybody.

To each [of you] the revelation of the Spirit is apportioned – to build up [the Church]. This person, through the Spirit, may have clever rhetoric apportioned to him, and another person rhetoric of 'knowledge', according to the same Spirit. Another person may have faith, in the same Spirit, while someone else has the gift of healing in the same Spirit, and another person the power to work miracles, another person prophecy, another discernment of spirits, another, different kinds of languages, and another the interpretation of languages. It is one and the same Spirit that empowers all these things, privately apportioning to each one as the Spirit wills.

You can see how all these different (and perhaps clashing) gifts might cause division in the Church. How do you prioritise the gifts, and how do you prevent

The application of love to the problem of spiritual gifts

14 1-25 Make a special thing of love, but be eager for [all] spiritual gifts, especially, however, that you should prophesy. For the person who speaks in a tongue does not speak to human beings but to God. For no one is listening, while the person speaks of mysteries in the Spirit. Whereas the one who prophesies speaks upbuilding, comfort, and consolation to human beings. The one who speaks in a tongue builds him- or herself up, whereas the one who prophesies builds up the [entire] Church.

I'd like all of you to speak in tongues; but I'd prefer you to prophesy. The one who prophesies is more important than the one who speaks in tongues (unless they interpret it), so that the church may receive 'upbuilding'.

See here, my brothers and sisters, if I come to you talking in tongues, how am I going to help you, unless I speak to you, either with a revelation or with knowledge or with prophecy or with teaching?

Similarly, inanimates that can give a sound, like a flute or a guitar, if they don't produce different notes, how will people know what tune is being played on the flute or the guitar?

Another example: if a trumpet gives an unclear signal, who will make ready for war? So with you: if you don't give a clear message, how will people know what is being said? You see, you'll just be talking to empty air. There's any number of kinds of languages in the world, and every one of them makes a sound; but if I don't know the sound's force, I'll be a foreigner to the speaker, and the speaker will be a foreigner to me.

So with you – if you are keen on the spiritual gifts, be keen on having lots of them, that you may build up the church. Therefore let the person who speaks in a tongue pray to interpret [it]. For if I pray in a tongue, my spirit prays, but my mind gets no profit. What then? I shall indeed pray in the Spirit, but I'll also pray in the mind. I shall sing praise in the Spirit, but also in my mind. For if you pronounce a blessing in the Spirit, [what about] the person who fills the rôle of the outsider? How will they [be able to] say their 'Amen' to your thanksgiving? Because they have no idea what you are saying. You do a very nice line in thanksgiving; but the other person is not 'built up'. Thank God, I speak in tongues more than any of you; but in church I'd prefer to speak five intelligible words, in order to instruct others, than a million words in a tongue.

Brothers and sisters, don't be childish in your thinking; you can be infants in regard to doing evil, but in your thinking [I want] you to be mature. In the Torah it is written,

> 'In strange tongues and on foreign lips shall I speak to this people,
> and even so they will not listen to me, says the Lord.'

So tongues function as a sign, not for believers but for unbelievers, while prophecy is a sign, not for unbelievers but for those who believe. Therefore if the entire Church gathers as a community in the same place, and they all speak in tongues, and outsiders or unbelievers come in, won't they say that you're all mad?

If, on the other hand, everyone prophesies, and some unbeliever or outsider comes in, they are convicted by everybody and judged by everybody, and the secrets of their heart are revealed, so that they fall on their face and worship God, proclaiming that 'Indeed God is among you.'

It is not having the spiritual gifts that makes the difference, but the use to which they are put: do they operate, as love always does, in a way that benefits the community ('upbuilding') and outsiders (bringing them to a knowledge of their need for God)?

What are your gifts for?

How to ensure 'upbuilding' in the Church

26-40 What about it, then, brothers and sisters? When you come together as a community, each one has a song, or a teaching, or a revelation, or a tongue, or an interpretation: let everything work for 'upbuilding'. If someone speaks in a tongue, [let it be] two or at most three, and in order; and let one [of them] interpret. If, however, there is no interpreter, let's have a bit of silence in the church, and let everyone speak to themselves and to God. And let two or three prophets speak, and let the rest discern. And if someone else gets a revelation, when they are sitting down, let the first one be silent. For you can all prophesy one by one, so that all may be instructed, and all be encouraged. And the prophets' spirits are under the control of the prophets; for God is not a God of unruliness but of peace.

As in all the churches of the saints, let wives refrain from speaking in the churches. For it is not permitted for them to speak; rather, let them be subordinated, as the Torah says. If, however, they wish to learn something, let them enquire of their own husbands at home. For it is a disgrace for a woman to speak in the assembly. Or is it from you people alone that the Word of God emerged? Was it to you people alone that it came?

If someone thinks that they are a prophet or spiritual, I want them to recognise that what I am writing to you is the Lord's command. If a person doesn't recognise this, they aren't recognised.

So, my brothers and sisters, be keen to prophesy, and don't put a bar on speaking in tongues. But let everything happen properly, and in good order.

This is all about avoiding liturgical chaos, a particular danger (presumably) for charismatics. The keyword here is 'upbuilding', which Paul has long since identified as the effect of love. And upbuilding will not take place if the liturgical celebration turns into a free-for-all. Clearly all that Paul says here is meant to subserve that basic end; and it is in that context that we must read the apparently rather forbidding injunction on women (or wives) to be 'silent in church'. We do not know the 'other side' of the conversation, but we must assume that both Paul and the Corinthians know the precise issue that he had in mind. There is some uncertainty about the manuscript tradition here, but on balance it is held that the teaching about women probably came from Paul.

It does not follow from this, of course, that Paul was enacting legislation whereby no woman, even in the third millennium, must open her mouth in the

Christian assembly. For one thing, Paul would have been rather surprised to know that we should still be reading his letter, written on a particular occasion, for the problems of a particular church, almost two thousand years later. For another, unless we can be sure what kind of anarchy he was attempting to avoid, we cannot confidently state what he is telling the Corinthian women not to do. As always with Paul, notice how he comes back to 'the Lord' at the end of his instructions.

'A bit of silence in the church'; what might Paul have meant by this?

The gospel as originally preached – a reminder

15 1-11 Fellow Christians, I am making known to you [again!] the gospel which I gospelled to you, which you received, on which you stand secure, through which you are being saved, the terms in which I gospelled you, if you still hold it fast (unless, of course, you came thoughtlessly to faith).

So, in the first place [you will recall], I passed on to you, what I had also received, that Christ

- died for our sins according to the scriptures;
- that he was buried;
- that he was raised on the third day according to the scriptures;
- and that he appeared to Kephas, then to the Twelve.

Then he appeared to more than five hundred brothers and sisters at once, of whom the majority still remain [alive], although some have fallen asleep. Then he appeared to James, and then to all the apostles. Last of all, as though to an abortion, he appeared also to me. I am, you see, the least of the apostles; I'm not fit to be called an 'apostle', because I persecuted God's Church. By God's grace, I am what I am, and God's grace towards me hasn't turned out unprofitably. Actually, I worked harder than all of them – not really me, though, so much as God's grace [working] with me. So, whoever, they or I, that's how we preach, and that's how you came to faith.

Paul turns here to a very different subject, that of resurrection, but for many scholars this is the climax of the letter, the point it has been aiming at from the beginning. We have to work out, from what Paul says, precisely what the Corinthians had got wrong; but it seems to have been (at least in Paul's view) a matter of denying the gospel as it had originally been preached to them. Some have called this the 'gospel of four verbs': Christ 'died', 'was buried', 'was raised', and 'appeared'. Paul is quite clear that it is a non-optional part of Christianity.

Why is the Resurrection so important to Paul? Is it still important today?

So what are some of you getting up to?

12-19 Now, if the proclamation is that Christ is raised from the dead, how is it that some among you are saying that there is no such thing as resurrection from the dead? But if there is no such thing as resurrection from the dead, then nor has Christ been raised. And if Christ has not been raised, then our proclamation is void, and your faith is void; and we turn out to be false witnesses for God, because we bore witness against God that he raised Christ, when [in fact] he didn't raise him [at all], if [it is really true that] the dead aren't raised. You see, if the dead aren't raised, then Christ wasn't raised, either. And if Christ wasn't raised, then your faith is futile, and you are still in your sins, and, moreover, those who have slept in Christ are lost. If in this [present] life our hope has been in Christ alone, then we are the most pitiable of all human beings.

Resurrection is the hardest thing to believe, 'news too good to be true', in some people's view, and quite clearly the Corinthians, or some of them, were finding it hard to believe that Christians they knew who had died, and whose rotting corpses were presumably available (at least in theory) for inspection in some Corinthian cemetery, might in any sense be said to be still alive. Paul takes them through the logic of their position: the heart of Christianity is the resurrection of Christ; but if there is no such thing as resurrection, then Christianity is built on a lie, and (what is worse) a slander against God. If that is the case, then their conversion was a fairy tale. Paul lays it all bare, and invites them to choose; and the invitation is extended to us also.

Which will you choose?

The structure of resurrection

20-28 As it is, however, Christ ***has*** been raised from the dead, the 'first-fruits' of those who have fallen asleep. For since [it was] through a human being that death [happened], it was also through a human being that the resurrection from the dead happened. That is to say, in Adam everybody dies, and in just the same way everybody will be brought to life, but each in their own order: Christ (as the first-fruits), then those who belong to Christ, at his coming. Then, finally, when he hands over the kingdom to the [one who is] God and Father, [comes the end] when he cancels out every rule and every authority and power. For it is required that he should reign until 'he place all enemies beneath his feet'. It is death that is the final enemy [to be] cancelled out. For 'he subjected everything under his feet'; however, when he says 'everything has been subjected', clearly that does not include the One who subjected everything to him. When he subjects everything to him, then the Son himself will be subjected to the one who subjected everything to him, in order that God may be all in all.

In this section, Paul traces the pattern of resurrection, and he picks up the parallel between Adam and Christ that we read in Romans 5, and extends it. The pattern is as follows: Adam brought in death; Christ is God's answer to death, which will be progressively eliminated from the universe; Christ, then Christians, then, finally, the whole of creation, as it is restored to the proper order that God designed, and which Adam shattered. All that is opposed to God will be defeated, and the final (and perhaps most intractable) enemy is going to be death, but death, too, will be defeated, and then the universe will once more be as it should be.

There is, however, one important difference: Christ has come into the picture. So far in this letter, we have seen that Paul gives Jesus a very high status indeed, calling him 'Lord', and clearly understanding by this some kind of equivalence to God. At this point, however, he moderates it somewhat, and as Christ hands over our restored universe to the Most High God, Paul makes it clear that the Son is also subject to God. The Christian community was only at the beginning (and perhaps we have not advanced much further) of the enquiry into how God and Christ are related.

Appeal to a Christian practice

29-34 Because what will those people be doing who get themselves baptised for the sake of the dead? If the dead aren't raised, why are they getting baptised for their sakes?

And what about us? Why do we take risks all day long? Every day I'm on the point of death. Yes – by the pride in you which I have in Christ Jesus our Lord! If (in human terms) I have fought with wild animals here in Ephesus, what's in it for me? If the dead aren't raised,

'Let's eat and drink, for tomorrow we die.'

Don't be fooled – 'Bad company corrupts even excellent morals.'

Sober up properly; stop sinning. Some people have an un-'knowledge' of God. I am speaking to shame you.

Paul now argues from what they know. First, from the practice of 'being baptised for the sake of the dead'. It has been estimated that there are some thirty explanations of what this might mean. All we can say for certain is that it was a practice that the Corinthians recognised, but which is absurd, unless the Christian proclamation of resurrection is true.

Next Paul appeals to his own experiences as an apostle: the risks he endures are clearly pointless unless it is true about resurrection. Then he offers a couple of quotations. The first may be from Isaiah 22:13, or from contemporary criticism of the Epicurean philosophers, and the second is from a Greek poet. Finally, perhaps feeling that he is running out of arguments, he adds a touch of asperity: 'get your act together'.

The obvious next question is: 'All right, then; what will resurrection **look** *like?' To that question Paul now turns; and the reader must judge whether or not he succeeds in finding the answer.*

What will Resurrection look like? Arguments from nature

35-58 But someone will object, 'How are the dead raised? What body do they come wearing?'

Fool – what you sow doesn't get turned into life unless it dies. In this instance, what you sow in the ground is not the body that will be, but a bare grain, as it might be of wheat, or one of those things. But God gives it 'body', as he intended, and each of the different seeds has its own 'body'. Not all flesh is identical. No – you have one kind for humans, another kind for cattle, another for birds, and another kind of flesh for fish. Then there are heavenly bodies and earthly bodies, and their glory is of two different kinds. The sun's glory is quite different from that of the moon; and that of the stars is different again. For different stars are different in their glory.

[Have you got that?] Well, that's how it is with the resurrection of the dead. A corpse is sown in corruption, and raised in un-corruption. A corpse is sown in dishonour, and raised in glory. A corpse is sown in weakness, and raised in power. A human body is sown; it is a spiritual body that is raised. If there is a human body, there is also such a thing as a spiritual body. So it is also written, 'The first man, Adam, came to be as a living human', [Genesis 2:7] while the final Adam came to be as a life-giving spirit.

However, the order is not spiritual first, but human first, then spiritual. The first human came from the earth, made of dust; the second human came from heaven.

As is the Person of Dust, so are his successors in dust; as is the Heavenly One, so are his successors from heaven. And as we have carried the likeness of the Person of Dust, so we shall carry the likeness of the Heavenly One.

This is what I mean, brothers and sisters: flesh and blood cannot inherit the kingdom of God; corruption does not inherit un-corruption. Look! I am telling you a mystery. We shall not all fall asleep; but we shall all be changed, in a nanosecond, in the blink of an eye – at the final trumpet.

For the trumpet will signal – and then the dead shall be raised undecayed. And for ourselves, we shall be changed. For this decaying part must put on un-decay, and this mortal part put on immortality. But when this decaying part puts on un-decay, and this mortal part puts on immortality, then the word of Scripture will come true: 'Death has been swallowed up into victory' [Isaiah 25:8]. 'Where, death, is [your] victory? Where, death, is your sting?' [Hosea 13:14].

The sting of death is sin; and the power of sin is the law. Thanks be to God who gives us the victory through our Lord Jesus Christ!

So, my beloved fellow Christians, be firm of purpose, unbudging, always doing all in your power in the Lord's work, knowing that – in the Lord – your labour is not useless.

We may not have followed every twist and turn of the argument here, but we should be heartened by Paul's massive certainties. Resurrection may indeed seem like 'news too good to be true'; but that is not a discovery of the twenty-first century – Paul has been there before us and faced the difficulty. What makes the difference for him is his certainty of the unfailing presence of Christ.

Do you think that Christians experience this 'unfailing presence'?

Arrangements for the collection

16 1-4 About the collection for the saints, as I instructed the churches of Galatia,
so you must do. On the first day of the week, let each of you put something

aside at home, saving up whatever fits in with how they are doing financially; this is to avoid doing the calculations when I come. But when I do come, I'll give a letter of introduction to whoever meets your criteria, to carry your generous gift to Jerusalem. And if it is appropriate for me to go too, they'll come with me.

The 'collection', for the impoverished Jerusalem Church, was of enormous importance for Paul. It is a statement for him of Christian solidarity. Those who are better off are, in his view, obliged to look after fellow Christians who are struggling materially. That is a part of what being Christian means – looking after the other bits of the Body, as he might have said in Chapter 12 above.

It may not be too fanciful to read here evidence of some lack of trust in the Corinthian Church. For, first, Paul tells them to 'put something aside' each Sunday, rather than (as we should expect) bringing it to church, to put in the collection. So perhaps the Corinthians could not even trust each other with charitable money. And, second, Paul is not at all sure whether they are prepared to allow him to escort the collection to Jerusalem. This Church is not at ease with itself, nor with its founder.

Paul's travel plans

5-9 I'll come to you when I pass through Macedonia. For I am passing through Macedonia, and perhaps I'll stay a while with you, and even spend the winter with you, so that you can send me on wherever I am going. For this time I don't want to see you just in passing; I'm hoping to remain quite a while with you, if the Lord permits. I'm staying at Ephesus until Pentecost, because a powerful door has opened wide for me – and several people are opposing me.

In the opening chapter of 2 Corinthians, we shall see that it looks as though Paul was over-optimistic here, and he never actually made it. All kinds of things could intervene in his missionary work. In winter, snow on land and storms at sea, as well as the various kinds of opposition he might encounter. In addition, Paul's deepest question was always 'What does Jesus want me to do now?', and that was not always identical to what the Corinthians might want him to do.

What normally dictates ***your*** *travel plans?*

Be nice to Timothy. Apollos won't be coming

10-12 If Timothy comes, make sure that he comes to you without cause for fear. For he is doing the Lord's work, just as I am. So don't let anyone disdain him; send him on his way in peace, for him to come to me. For I'm waiting for him, with the Christians here.

With regard to our brother Apollos, I begged and begged him to come to you with the other brothers and sisters, but it was definitely not his [or: **God's**] wish that he should come to you at this moment. He will come when the time is right.

There is a hint of unease in these verses also. Paul is quite menacing as he tries to ensure that Timothy is received properly, reminding them that he will soon find out whether or not they did the right thing. He does not tell us why the Corinthians might not receive Timothy properly; it may have been a general sense of 'We want the organ-grinder, not his monkey.' And Apollos's absence also suggests looming mistrust; some may have thought that Paul was preventing him from coming because he was the leader of a faction opposed to Paul. Or it may have been (more piously) that Apollos was so horrified at having his name used by a particular splinter group in Corinth that he thought it better to leave it awhile. It is striking, however, that Paul does not make it clear whose will it wasn't for Apollos to come to Corinth (Apollos? Paul? God?).

Final greetings

13-24 Stay awake; stand firm in the faith; be courageous; grow in strength. Let all your business be done in love.

One thing I'm asking of you, brothers and sisters. You know Stephanas's household – they were the first converts in Asia, and they have set themselves to serve the saints. I want you people to be subject to people like this, and to all collaborators and workers. I'm really happy at the presence of Stephanas and Fortunatus and Achaicus; because these are people who have made up for the lack of you, for they refreshed both my spirits and yours. So – give recognition to people of this sort.

The churches of Asia greet you. Aquila and Prisca greet you in the Lord, along with the church that meets in their house. All the Christians here greet you. Greet each other with a holy kiss.

Here's the greeting in my hand: PAUL

If anyone doesn't love the Lord, let him or her be accursed.

Marana Tha.

The grace of Our Lord Jesus be with you.

My love be with all of you in Christ Jesus.

There is a breathlessness about the last lines of the letter, and no let-up in the tension. The conclusion begins with a reminder of certain virtues that they had been ignoring in Corinth. It continues with what is presumably a reprimand for their lack of respect for the 'household of Stephanas', whose name suggests that he may have been a freedman, and perhaps therefore not taken seriously by the Corinthian Christians, despite his evident good will.

Then come the usual greetings: 'The churches of Asia send you their love' might capture the mood a bit better than my translation does. The reference to Aquila and Prisca reminds us that Acts 18 has Paul working and living in Corinth with this husband and wife team, who were also responsible for capturing the gifted Apollos.

As usual, Paul makes his mark on the papyrus of the letter, with an insistence on 'loving the Lord', and an Aramaic prayer, 'Our Lord, come', and a characteristic conclusion, where Jesus is twice mentioned, and love is given its proper place.

So ends perhaps Paul's most remarkable letter.

The Second Letter to the Corinthians

The Second Letter to the Corinthians

Opening greeting

1 1,2 Paul, apostle of Jesus Christ through the will of God, and Timothy our fellow
Christian, to the Church of God which is in Corinth, along with all the saints
who are in the whole of Achaia. Grace to you and peace, from God our Father and
the Lord Jesus Christ.

This is an entirely characteristic opening to a Pauline letter; notice his distinctive emphasis that his vocation as an apostle is 'through the will of God'; his mention of Timothy (1 Corinthians 16:10-11 appears to suggest that they had been less than respectful of him); the extension of the greeting beyond the confines of Corinth to 'the whole of Achaia'; Paul's use of the words 'grace' and 'peace', which are very important elements in his understanding of what God has done in Christ; and, finally, the mention, virtually in the same breath, of God the Father and Jesus. All of this sets the scene for what is to follow.

This is perhaps Paul's most passionate and emotional letter. In consequence, it is very often hard to see precisely what he is saying, and the sound of the Greek is jerky and at times impenetrable. The translation has left Paul obscure where he has been obscure (generally noting when this was the case); but the reader needs to be assured that no disrespect is thereby intended to the apostle.

Thanksgiving

3-7 Blessed be the God and Father of our Lord Jesus Christ, the Father of mercies
and the God of all comfort, who comforts us in all our affliction, so that we can comfort
people in all [kinds of] distress, through the comfort with which we ourselves have
been comforted by God. Because just as Christ's sufferings overflow to us, so,
through Christ, our comfort also overflows. If we are being afflicted [it is] for your
comfort and salvation. If we are being comforted, it is for your comfort, which works
itself out in enduring the same sufferings that we are undergoing. And our expecta-
tion for you is solidly based; we know that just as you are partners in the suffering, so
also [you will be partners] in the comfort.

Notice the tension here, between 'comfort' and 'affliction'. In one guise or another, this will run through all of the letter; at present the reader does not know, although presumably the Corinthians who first heard this letter read out did know, what are the 'afflictions' for which comfort is on offer. But clearly there is a continuity between the sufferings of Christ, those of Paul, and whatever the Corinthians were currently having to put up with. Notice also the word 'partners', which translates two words that are familiar from 1 Corinthians, koinonos *and* koinonia, *which refer to ideas like partnership, union, communion, and solidarity. And, as in the opening of 1 Corinthians, the series of passive verbs may carry a warning to the Corinthians not to pride themselves too much.*

Does God always 'comfort' us in our 'afflictions'? If so, in what ways?

Some unidentifiable troubles

8-11 My fellow Christians, we do not want you to be ignorant of the affliction that happened to us in Asia, [when] we were weighed down, far beyond our resources. The result was that we even despaired of living; we actually had the death sentence on us; this was so that we should not trust in ourselves, but in God who raises up the dead. God is the one who rescued us from so great a [danger of] death, and will rescue us again; that is the God in whom we still hope that he will rescue us once more, as long as you join in helping us with your prayers, in order that thanksgiving may be made on our behalf from many people, because of the favour granted to us through many prayers.

The translation of the last sentence is, frankly, anyone's guess; and indeed, for what we know, it is anyone's guess what the life-threatening troubles were to which Paul refers, though evidently he expected the Corinthians to know. They may be hinted at in 1 Corinthians 15:32; 16:9, and in the account in Acts 19 of the riots in Ephesus. What comes out with absolute clarity is Paul's total dependence on God, his insistence on the Resurrection, and his affirmation of the importance of prayer as something that Christians do for each other.

How does prayer work for Christians?

Boasting: only in God, and in Jesus Christ

12-14 For this is our boast, the witness that our conscience bears, that we have conducted ourselves in the world, more especially towards you, with the simplicity and purity of God, not by human cleverness, but by God's grace. For all we write to you is nothing other than what you read, and what you recognise. And my hope is that you will [continue to] recognise to the end, just as you partly recognised us, that we are your boast, just as you are our boast on the day of our Lord Jesus.

Look out for the idea of boasting in this letter; this section, obviously, begins and ends with it; we shall see it again. Probably we may read 'between the lines' here, that the Corinthians have been complaining about Paul. They may well have been complaining that he is different in person to how he presents himself in his letters.

What does Paul mean by 'boasting' here?

Paul's abandoned travel plans

15-22 It was with this confidence that I was wanting to come to you before, for you to have a second chance of the gift; [the idea was] to come via you to Macedonia, and then to come back to you again after Macedonia, and have you send me on my way to Judaea. So when I was planning this, was I 'behaving irresponsibly'? [Are you saying that] my decision was an unspiritual decision, so that in my case 'yes' should mean 'yes' and 'no' should mean 'no'?

It is God who is reliable: our word to you is not 'yes-and-no'. For the Son of God, Jesus Christ, the one who was proclaimed among you through us, that is to say through me and Silvanus and Timothy, wasn't 'yes-and-no' but 'yes'. For as many as are the promises of God, in [Jesus they find their] 'yes'. So it is through him that the 'Amen' is [given] to God for glory, through our [preaching]. It is God who confirms us – along with you – into Christ; and God who anoints us; God who gives us the certificate of authenticity, and who provides the 'down-payment' of the Spirit of God in our hearts.

Clearly there have been complaints from Corinth (for another example, later in the letter, see 2 Corinthians 10:1, 10, 11); and the ground for complaint is that in 1 Corinthians 16:5-9 Paul said that he would come, and never turned up. They seem to have accused him of irresponsibility and selfishness ('unspiritual decision') and vacillation. Paul is not pleased, that much is clear; but notice how, as always, he brings the question back to God and to Jesus Christ, or to God-in-Jesus-Christ. There is an untranslatable pun towards the end of this section, when Paul speaks of Christ ('The Anointed One' or 'Messiah'), and then, immediately afterwards, of 'God who anoints us'. His apostolate, he never tires of saying, is from God, as is Christ's mission. If they don't like it, it is Christ they have to blame, not Paul.

When is it permissible for Christians not to keep their promises?

Paul's attitude to the Corinthian Christians

1 23–2 4 I call on God as my witness (I stake my life on it) that it was in order to spare you that I did not after all come to Corinth. This was not because we lord it over your faith. No – we are working with you, to bring you joy. For it is by faith that you stand.

For my decision was not to return to you in grief. For if I cause you grief, who is to cheer me up, other than the one whom I have grieved? And this is the reason why I wrote this letter: [I didn't want to] come and have grief from the ones who ought to bring me joy. I am convinced with regard to all of you that my joy is that of you all. It was out of great affliction and anguish of heart that I wrote to you, with many tears; [I didn't want] you to grieve, but to know the love I have especially for you.

There had obviously been a major breakdown in relations between Paul and the Christians in Corinth, and both sides have been upset. Paul is here trying to rebuild the relationship, without retreating from whatever position it was that he had adopted. Quite clearly he is very fond of his Corinthians, even when they irritate him.

Can we be fond of people, and at the same time irritated by them?

Punishing (but with love) a person who has done wrong

5-11 If someone has caused grief, it wasn't to me that they caused it, but to all of you, in a way (I don't want to exaggerate). For a person like that this punishment is appropriate, at the hands of the majority, so that – on the contrary – you should rather forgive the person and comfort them; we don't want a person like that to be overwhelmed with greater grief. So I'm encouraging you to reaffirm your love for that person. This was the reason I wrote, to know your quality, to see if you are obedient in every respect. If you forgive someone, so do I: for any forgiveness that I have granted (if I ***have*** granted any), is for your sakes, in the person of Christ. We don't want to be outwitted by Satan; for we are well aware of Satan's intentions.

The translation is tricky here; to follow what is going on, and to decide how to take some of the Greek words and phrases that Paul uses, we would need to hear both ends of the 'telephone conversation' at once. Without that, the translation depends on interpretative guesswork. Clearly someone (perhaps the incestuous person of 1 Corinthians 5:1, or perhaps a visitor from elsewhere who has challenged Paul's right to be an apostle) has done something that requires drastic measures in response; Paul regards the offence (whatever it was) as utterly evil, the work of Satan, and, clearly, he was not too pleased with how the Corinthians had coped with it. And, in all probability, someone has been questioning Paul's authority, which is never a good idea.

What do you think 'Satan's intentions' might be?

A slightly mysterious travel detail

12, 13 When I came to Troas, for the gospel of Christ, and because a door opened for me in the Lord, I could not relax spiritually, because I didn't find Titus, my fellow Christian. Instead, I said goodbye to them, and left for Macedonia.

Troas is a regular port from which to leave Asia Minor for Europe (see Acts 16:11, and consult a map); so clearly Paul was on his way to Corinth after some arrangements had broken down. Once again, we cannot be clear what has happened, but he seems still to be referring to his failure to come to Corinth (which was partly through a desire not to cause more pain).

God's is the victory; and Paul is God's apostle

14-17 Thanks be to God, who always leads us in triumph in Christ, and who always makes known the fragrance of the knowledge of him, through us, everywhere we go. Because we are Christ's 'sweet scent' to God, among those who are being saved, and among those who are being lost. For some it is a scent that leads them from death to death; for others, it is a smell that leads from life to life – and who is equal to this [task]? For we aren't (as many people are) putting God's word up for sale. No – it is with pure motives that we speak in Christ. No – it is from God and before God that we speak.

Once again we should very much like to know what those Corinthians knew; they must have understood precisely what he was telling them. Paul uses a metaphor ('lead in triumph') from a Roman victory parade, which shows him to be God's willing prisoner; he then uses (almost battering it into the ground) another (the sweet smell of sacrifices) from Old Testament religion. Both of these images emphasise how God and Christ are at the heart of Paul's life and ministry. He sees his ministry as a daunting task, but one that he thinks he is at least performing with integrity. And it is a matter of 'life and death'.

What is Paul's relation to Christ, and to God? Try and reach your answer from what he writes in this section.

From the Corinthian complaints to Paul's ministry

3 1-3 Are we starting to 'commend ourselves' again? Surely we don't need any letters of recommendation, either to you or from you! ***You*** are our letter, a letter written on our hearts, known and read by everyone; you are revealed to be Christ's letter, served up by us, written not in ink but in the Spirit of the Living God, not on stone tablets, but on the tablets of hearts of flesh.

Implicit in the complaints that the Corinthians have evidently been making is a protest about how Paul has been approaching his ministry, and possibly also about his reaction to criticism – the idea of 'commending oneself' will appear again and again in this letter, and may have been a quotation from his Corinthian opponents. Paul has heard their protest, and now shifts, almost imperceptibly, into a defence of his apostolate. But it is not just prickly defensiveness; as we shall see in what follows, Paul is now thinking his way through his theory of what it is to be an apostle, and what it is to be a church. What comes next is an account of what God is doing in Christ, and in Paul, and why it matters, for Corinth, and for the world at large. The idea of the letter 'known and read' by everyone, contains another untranslatable pun: see 1:13. The metaphor of a letter may perhaps have been suggested by what Paul was actually doing, and perhaps reflects his discovery of just how powerful a letter can be as a means of communication.

What does Paul mean by calling his Corinthian Christians a 'letter'?

The ministry of the living God

4-11 We have as much confidence as this in God through Christ. It is not that we are sufficient from our own resources, to credit anything as coming from us. No – our resources come from God, who has given us the resources to be ministers of the New Covenant, which is a covenant not of the letter but of the Spirit. For the letter kills, but the Spirit gives life.

If the ministry of death, carved in stone letters, made its appearance in radiance, so that the children of Israel were unable to look on the face of Moses, because of the transient nature of the radiance of his face, will not the ministry of the Spirit all the more appear in radiance?

If the ministry [that led to] condemnation had its own radiance, all the more will the ministry of righteousness be saturated in radiance. You see, that which has been endowed with radiance is not in this case given radiance because of its own surpassing radiance. If that which is transient has radiance, how much more that which is permanent?

If you did not understand a word of this, don't worry; it is not easy, and scholars are divided about what it might mean. What is clear is that Paul is emphasising the superiority of the New Covenant to the old. Once again, we see his insistence that it is life over death; and on the side of life, Paul speaks of spirit and of righteousness.

Why could the children of Israel not look on Moses' face? Because he had been close to God (see Exodus 34:29-35); and, some scholars suggest, the children of Israel had already indicated that they didn't want to get too close to the living God (see Exodus 20:18-21).

What has this got to do with Paul and his Corinthians? They need to accept this opportunity for direct access to the New Covenant of the Living God, and willingly.

What do you think was wrong with the 'Old Covenant', according to Paul?

Unrestrained access to God

12-18 So since we have a hope as great as this, let us behave with great boldness. Let's not be like Moses, who put a veil on his face, so that the children of Israel should not look upon the end of what was transitory. Instead, their thoughts were hardened. Right up to the present day, there is still the same veil at the reading of the Old Covenant; the veil is not lifted up, because in Christ [the Old Covenant] is transitory.

Instead, right down to today, whenever Moses is read, a veil lies over their hearts. 'But whenever he turned to the Lord, the veil was lifted' [Exodus 34:34]. Now the Lord is the Spirit, and where there is the Spirit of the Lord, there is freedom. But all of us, with uncovered faces contemplating [or: 'reflecting'] the Lord's radiance, are transformed from radiance into radiance, as from the Spirit of the Lord.

This is still difficult to follow; but a few things are clear:

- *'boldness' is an important idea. The children of the New Covenant enjoy (and should make use of) unrestrained access to God;*
- *Moses' veiled face prevents the children of Israel from encountering God's radiance, and from seeing that the Old Covenant is transitory;*
- *Jesus, on the other hand, is the likeness of God; and Paul has gazed on that likeness – but the radiance is not to be hidden. Instead, there is the opportunity for all to be transformed;*
- *Spirit, Lord, Jesus, God, are all part-names for the bright reality that is being offered;*
- *we may also notice how, in this letter, Paul makes use of the metaphor of 'letter'. In 3:1 he contrasts 'letters of recommendation' with the living 'letter' that the Corinthians are, a 'letter of Christ', written not in ink but in the*

Spirit of the Living God, on the heart, not on stone tablets (and we think of Ezekiel 36:26). Later on he will refer to 'The Letter' (7:8), which caused them pain, and is part of the history of their complicated relationship. Chapter 3:6 contrasts 'writing' and 'Spirit', and verses 7 and 8 contrast stone-death with radiance-life. Verse 9 drifts from the metaphor, but note how the contrast continues: condemnation-righteousness. In verses 14 and 15, the metaphor of 'letter' recurs with the idea of 'reading'. We have unrestrained access, and the access can transform us.

This is difficult material, but the broad landmarks are clear enough.

'Let us behave with great boldness'. What are Christians being encouraged to do here?

No veil over our hearts

4 1-6 Because of this, since we have this ministry, just as we have received mercy, we do not lose heart; instead, we have renounced the things that we hide out of shame. We do not behave in a crafty manner; we do not falsify God's word. Instead, we recommend ourselves to the conscience of all people before God, by revealing the Truth. If our gospel is a hidden one, it is [only] hidden for those who are on the way to destruction, those among whom the god of this age has blinded the thoughts of unbelievers, so that they do not see the gospel's illumination, the radiance of Christ, who is the likeness of God.

We do not, you see, preach ourselves, but the Lord Jesus Christ, and ourselves as your slaves because of Jesus. For it is God who said, 'out of darkness light shall shine'; and that is the God who has shone in our hearts, to illuminate the knowledge of the radiance of God, in the person [or face] of Jesus Christ.

To grasp what is going on here, it is important to see that Paul is still thinking of the experience of the children of Israel in the desert. He seems to be saying that because they did not want to see the living God, Moses wore a veil, which also had the effect of hiding from them the fact that the dispensation was not going to last. Now, however, the vision is available, because Christ is the likeness of God, and God can therefore be known, and the world ('all people') transformed.

'Christ, who is the likeness of God'. What do you think Paul meant by this?

The power is God's, not ours

7-18 But we hold this treasure in clay pots, so that the immense power should be [seen to be] from God and not from us.

In every way we are afflicted, but not crushed; we are perplexed, but not despairing. We are persecuted, but not utterly abandoned, struck down but not destroyed, always carrying around Jesus' putting-to-death in our body, so that Jesus' life might be revealed in our body.

For all the time we who are alive are being handed over to death because of Jesus, so that Jesus' life may be revealed in our mortal flesh.

The result is that death is doing its work in us, but life in you. We have the same Spirit of faith, according to the scripture, 'I believed, and so I spoke.' In just the same way, we believe, and so we speak, knowing that the one who raised the Lord Jesus will raise us also with Jesus and will set us before him, along with you.

For everything is because of you, in order that increasing grace may, through the thanksgiving of the many, overflow to the radiance [or: glory] of God.

So [as I say] we do not lose heart; no – even if our outer being is wasting away, our inner being keeps being renewed, day in and day out.

For the present light weight of our affliction is bringing about an incomparable, immeasurable, solid weight of glory for us. We keep our eyes, not on the things that are visible, but on the things that are invisible; for visible things are just temporary, while invisible things are eternal.

Now, you may feel, we are emerging into the sunlight, and that difficult passage in the last chapter starts to make sense. As always, Paul's eyes are on God, not on himself; hence the contrast between the 'treasure' and the 'clay pots' in which the treasure is contained. The clay pots represent apostles for Paul; but the attention of Paul and of his Corinthians must always be on the glory of God. This 'glory' is invisible, but it exercises an unmistakably transforming power – Paul clearly expected to be able to see it make a difference.

The word that I have translated as 'radiance' is often rendered as 'glory'; the reader needs to have both ideas in mind.

Notice how important resurrection is in Paul's thinking. It seems to him entirely appropriate that he and his fellow-ministers should be suffering, because the same God who raised Jesus from the dead is still at work, bringing out the 'glory' that (at the moment) can't quite be seen.

What are the 'things that are invisible'?

God is working our transformation

5 1-10 For we know that when our earthly home [which is no more than a tent] is destroyed, we have a building from God, a house not made by hand, eternal, in heaven. For in our present [home] we are groaning, longing to put on, over the top, our home from heaven. That is, assuming that once we strip off we shall not turn out to be naked. For while we are in the tent, we groan and are weighed down, because we do not want to strip off, but to put on additional clothing, so that what is deathly in us may be swallowed up by life. It is God who is working on us for this very purpose, God who gives us the down-payment of the Spirit.

So let us always take courage, and know that when we are at home in the body we are away from the Lord. The thing is, it is through faith that we proceed, not through outward appearance. We take courage, and we prefer to be away from the body and at home with the Lord. Therefore it is our ambition, whether at home or away, to be pleasing to him. For all of us must appear before Christ's tribunal, so that each one may receive a reward for the things they have done through the body, whether good or evil.

For Paul, resurrection is central and indispensable to the gospel. This means looking beyond what is present and tangible. It is not something we can take for granted (we might easily miss out on it) – but we can be confident that God is unceasingly at work to bring about resurrection. How do we know? As far as Paul is concerned, it is through the Spirit, a palpable presence. Have we lost something here?

The reference to Christ's tribunal may remind the alert reader about the tribunal in Corinth before which Paul was hauled, according to Acts 18:12. More than that, it may serve as a reminder that Jesus is Judge for Paul; that is to say, he is (yet again) taking over a function hitherto reserved for God.

The 'down-payment of the Spirit'. What does Paul mean by this (which also appears at 1:22)?

What God-in-Christ has done; what the Corinthians should do

11-21 So, since we know the fear of the Lord, we are trying to persuade human beings – to God we are transparent. But I hope that we are transparent also to your consciences. We are not (once more) 'recommending ourselves' to you, but giving you an incentive for boasting about us, so that you may have [something to say] to those who boast about appearances, and not in the heart. For if we are 'out of our minds', it is for God; if we are in a calm state, that is for you. For Christ's love constrains us. Our verdict is this: if one has died on behalf of all, then all have died. And he died for all, in order that those who live might no longer live to themselves, but to the one who died for them and was raised.

So then: from now on, we regard nobody from a worldly point of view. Even if we knew Christ in the flesh, we no longer do so. The result is that if someone is 'in Christ', they are a new creation. What is old has passed away – look, [the] new has come! Everything comes from God, who, through Christ, reconciled us to himself, and who gave us this ministry of reconciliation. That is, that God was in Christ reconciling the world to himself, not reckoning their transgressions to them, and putting his message of reconciliation in us.

So we are Christ's ambassadors: [imagine] that God is pleading through us. On Christ's behalf we ***implore*** you: be reconciled to God. [Christ] who had no knowledge of sin, God made into 'sin' for our sakes, so that in Christ we should become God's righteousness.

Even in translation, Paul's passion is unmistakable here. What is he trying to get the Corinthians to do? **Not** *to admire Paul, but to 'be reconciled to God'. Some of them may have dismissed him, perhaps because he is so passionate about Christ, as 'out of his mind'; but as far as Paul is concerned, he is speaking of the deepest reality of all, God's Resurrection victory over Death; and that deepest reality is not just a gift to Jesus. It is available to transform the lives of absolutely everybody, such is God's generosity. But God will not force us. So 'be reconciled to God', says Paul to the Corinthians (dressing up as 'God's diplomat', although not perhaps in diplomatic language) and be astonished at God's generosity: he made Christ into 'sin', all for us!*

'Even if we knew Christ in the flesh, we no longer do so.' What do you think Paul is saying here?

What do you think Paul means by saying that God made Christ into 'sin'?

Paul's plea

6 1-10 So we are working along with you, and we beg you not to make God's gift useless, once you have accepted it. You know how he says, 'At the acceptable time I listened to you, and on the day of salvation I helped you' [Isaiah 49:8]. Look! ***Now*** is the beautifully acceptable time! Look! ***Now*** is the day of salvation! We do not give any occasion of offence, so that our ministry should not be censured. Instead, in every respect, we 'commend ourselves' as ministers of God: we put up with much affliction, calamities, difficulties, floggings, imprisonment, political disturbance, hard work, nights without sleep, days without food. We endure in sincerity and knowledge, in patience and decency, in the Holy Spirit, in unfeigned love, in speaking the truth, in the power of God. Our means are the armour of righteousness, to right and to left, through glory and dishonour, through ill repute and good repute. [We are regarded] as deceitful – and yet we are true; as unrecognised – and yet we are known; as dying – and look! we are alive; as punished – and yet not put to death; as distressed – and yet always rejoicing; as beggars – and yet we make many people rich; as having nothing – and yet possessing everything.

There is no main verb in the list of disasters and triumphs that starts with 'We do not give any occasion of offence'; so even saying 'we' here is only an intelligent guess at translating a string of participles. It is clear, though, what Paul is saying: seen in the light of the Resurrection, his ministry (and presumably that of Silvanus and Timothy also) is not the string of catastrophes that his opponents are suggesting. Clearly Paul's life as an apostle has been an eventful one, though it is beyond us to reconstruct exactly what it had involved, or to fit his account with what is reported in Acts.

What is Paul saying here about his apostolate?

The plea resumed (after the dramatic autobiographical interlude)

11-13 We have spoken openly to you, Corinthians; you have a place in our affections. It is not in us that you are cramped, but in your own emotions. In return, open yourselves also up to us (I am speaking as [a father speaks] to children).

Avoid anything that is not the living God

6 14–7 1 Don't get mismated with unbelievers; for what do righteousness and lawlessness have in common? How can light and darkness be partners? Can Christ and Beliar sing in harmony? What has a believer in common with an unbeliever? What agreement can there be between the Temple of God and idols? You see, we are the Temple of the living God, as God said,

'I shall dwell and walk among them
and I shall be their God and they shall be my people.'
Therefore 'Come out of the midst of them and be separated,' says the Lord, and
'Do not touch what is unclean
and I shall welcome you
and I shall be as a Father to you
and you shall be as sons and daughters to me,'
says the Lord Almighty.

So, my dear ones, since we have these promises, let us purify ourselves from every defilement of flesh and spirit, bringing about sanctification by the fear of God.

It is not altogether easy here to know what target Paul has in mind, and some scholars, noting that the previous section and that which follows flow easily into each other, have suggested that it is an interpolation, perhaps part of another letter that Paul wrote to his Corinthians. For a variety of reasons it seems better to read it here as Christians have read it for twenty centuries, and to admit that while we cannot be clear precisely what Paul has in view, the Corinthians will have been in no doubt.

When Paul tells the Corinthians not to get 'mismated with unbelievers', it is undeniably strong language – but it is what he wrote.

The three quotations above are from Exodus 29:45; Isaiah 52:11 and 43:6 respectively.

What does Paul want his Corinthians to do here?

The plea resumed

2-4 Make room for us. There is nobody we have wronged, nobody we have ruined, nobody we have taken advantage of. What I say is not to condemn [anybody]; for I have already said that you are in our hearts, to live and die together. I have great confidence in you; I boast a good deal about you; I am filled with comfort, and overflowing with joy, after all our affliction.

Reviewing their intimate and painful relationship

5-16 For when we came into Macedonia, our flesh had no rest – we were afflicted in every respect, with assaults from outside and fears within. But God, who comforts the lowly, comforted us through Titus's arrival, and not just his arrival, but also the comfort he had received in regard to you. He reported to us your longing for us, your grieving, and your enthusiastic support for me – so that I rejoiced all the more.

Because even if I caused you pain by 'The Letter', I don't feel any regret. Even if I had had some regret (because I observe that 'That Letter' caused you pain, even if it was only for a while), now I'm glad, not because you experienced pain, but because your pain led to your repenting. The pain you felt was in God's way, so that in no respect did you lose anything at our hands, because pain that is in God's way leads to repentance, and to salvation that is [certainly] not to be regretted. Whereas the world's pain brings about death. Look what this very business of being pained 'in God's way' has brought about in you, how much eagerness – but also a desire to defend yourselves, but also some indignation, but also some fear, but also some longing, but also some zeal, but also some vindication. In every respect, you 'commend yourselves' to be innocent in the affair.

So then, even if I did write to you, it wasn't because of the person who had done wrong, nor because of the person who had been wronged, but because of this eagerness of yours that has been shown on our behalf, before God. Because of this we have been comforted.

In addition to the comfort we received, we rejoiced even 'abundantlier' at Titus's joy – because his spirit was refreshed by all of you. Because if I had boasted to him a bit about you, I wasn't embarrassed. Instead, as we told you, just as we had told you the truth in every respect, so also our boasting before Titus came true. And his heart goes out to you all the more abundantly when he remembers the obedience you all showed, how you welcomed him 'with fear and trembling'. I'm delighted that in every respect I can count on you.

This is an extraordinarily warm and intimate passage, from this most emotional of Paul's letters. His affection is plain to see, even as he admits that there have been difficulties. Notice how all the time Paul brings the issue back to God, and what God is doing in the situation.

The syntax in the last-but-one sentence of the second paragraph is very hard to represent in English in any satisfactory way, and is a poor representation, but the best that I can do, of Paul's use of a conjunction that means something like 'but', only rather stronger.

The horrid word 'abundantlier' is an attempt to express Paul's rather ungrammatical enthusiasm.

Is it sometimes appropriate for Christians to cause each other pain?

The collection

8 1-24 I am letting you know, brothers and sisters, [about] God's collection [literally: 'grace'; see also 1 Corinthians 16:3], which was given by the churches of Macedonia, because it was through trial and much affliction that the overflowing of their joy and their profound poverty overflowed into the wealth of their simplicity; because I am witness that of their own accord, in line with what they could manage, and even beyond what they could manage, they begged us, most earnestly, for the grace and communion of the ministry to the saints, not as we had expected – instead, they gave themselves in the first place to the Lord, and to us through the will of God. The result was that we asked Titus, just as he had already made a beginning, so he would also complete this work of generosity among you.

But, as you overflow in every way, in faith and rhetoric, and knowledge and all eagerness, and in the love among you that comes from us, may you abound also in this work of grace. I am not saying this as a command, but through the eagerness of others, and testing the genuineness of your love; for you know the grace of our Lord

Jesus Christ, that because of us he became poor although he was rich, so that you might be rich through his poverty. And let me give you my opinion in this matter; this is for your benefit. A year ago you had already begun, not just to act but also to want to act; now bring the action to completion, so that your enthusiastic wanting may be matched by our bringing it to completion (so far as you are able). For if the enthusiasm is there, it is acceptable in proportion to what a person has, not in proportion to what a person does not have.

The idea is not that other people should get relief, while you get affliction; it is a question of equalisation – your present surplus balanced against their present need. Then their surplus may assist your need, so that there may be equalisation, as it is written,

'The one who [gathered] much did not have a surplus;
the one who [gathered] little did not go in want.'

Thanks be to God, who put into Titus's heart this eagerness for you, because he accepted the request; but because he was so very eager, of his own initiative he went off to [visit] you.

Along with him we sent the Christian, who is [widely] commended in all the churches [for his service to] the gospel. Not only that, but he was appointed by the churches as our travelling-companion, for this collection that was served up by us to the glory of God himself, and our good will. We tried to avoid anyone finding fault with us because of this lavish gift that is being served up by us; for we took careful thought, about not just how the Lord might see it, but also about how humans might see it. With them we sent that fellow Christian of ours, whose quality we have frequently tested, in many different circumstances: he is in earnest, and much more so now, with great confidence in you. If there is any problem about Titus, he is my partner and a fellow worker as far as you are concerned. If [about] our brethren, they are apostles of the churches, the glory of Christ. So give them proof of your love, and of our boasting on your behalf, in the presence of the churches.

The collection was of enormous importance to Paul, not just for the relief it brought to Christians in Jerusalem, who had no access to the welfare system that Jewish inhabitants operated there. The importance was also theological: this is how we do things in the Body of Christ. So we notice the number of 'theologically weight-bearing' terms that he uses here, and their flexibility. The word for 'collection' is the word he uses also for God's 'grace', for 'generosity', and even for 'thanks'. In addition he uses the root of the words for 'ministry' (which I have translated also as 'served up' and 'administered'), 'affliction', 'simplicity' (see 2 Corinthians 1:12; 8:2; 9:11, 13; 11:3, and not much used outside this letter, so it is clearly a term of some importance for this situation), 'comfort' (also translated as 'beg' or 'ask'), and 'communion' ('fellowship' or 'solidarity'). See how many other words you can see that are frequent in 2 Corinthians. Paul's theological insight here is: if this is how God has acted towards us in Christ, that is how we should act towards others who are 'in Christ'.

The 'equalisation' quotation, 'the one who [gathered] much did not have a surplus . . .' is from Exodus 16:18, where it refers to God's astonishing (and very precise) generosity with the manna. The point here is that Paul is trying to encourage the Corinthians to live out their generous desires, and not to fear that they will thereby be deprived.

There are occasional signs of haste here, and it is sometimes difficult to translate individual elements with any confidence; but the overall meaning is clear. Notice (as in 1 Corinthians 16) the occasional hints that the Corinthians may not quite trust Paul in financial matters. We have no very clear idea who is the 'Christian' or 'fellow Christian' of whom Paul speaks.

What is so important about the collection?

A reminder to be generous in the collection

9 1-15 As regards the ministry to the saints, it is superfluous for me to write to you. For I am well aware of your eagerness (about which I have boasted to the Macedonians!), that Achaia has been all ready since last year; and your ardour spurred most of them on. But I sent the brethren, so that our boasting about you might not prove hollow – I wanted you to be all ready, as I had told them. I didn't want us (never mind you!) to be embarrassed by this confidence, for example if some Macedonians accompanied you and found you unprepared! So it was necessary for me to ask those brethren to go on ahead to you and make the advance arrangements for the generosity that you had previously promised, [so that it would] be ready, like an act of generosity, and not [as something reluctantly conceded] by greedy people.

[Think of] this: the one who sows sparingly will also reap sparingly, and the one who sows generously will also reap generously. Each one as he has decided in advance, not sadly or under compulsion, for God loves a cheerful giver. For God is strong enough to overflow every kind of grace on you, so that always and in every way you may have enough of everything, and you may overflow into every kind of good deed. As it is written,

'He scattered, he gave to the poor;
his righteousness remains for ever' [Psalm 112:9].

The one who organises 'seed for the sower and bread for food' will also organise and increase your seed, and multiply the produce of your righteousness. [You will be] enriched into total simplicity, which brings about thanksgiving to God through us. Because the ministry of this service doesn't just provide for the needs of the saints, but also overflows through much thanksgiving to God. Through the quality of this ministry, [you are] glorifying God in the obedience of your confession of faith in the gospel of Christ, and by the simplicity of your solidarity with them and with all. And by their prayer for you they long for you because of the exceptional grace of God [that has come] upon you. Thanks be to God for his inexpressible gift.

Once again, Paul is utterly passionate in what he is saying here, and occasionally he is dictating so fast that we can see what he is saying, but not

quite how it fits together. The second and third sentences from the end, for example, are completely without a main verb in Greek.

The collection is of huge importance to Paul, and, as before, there are many words that we have already recognised as important in the letter: ministry, superfluity (also overflow or abundance), eagerness, boasting, ardour, promise, grief, quality, thanks (or grace), glory, simplicity, fellowship (or communion or solidarity), and the whole notion of generosity: Christians should act as God has acted towards them. That is how the transforming power of God-in-Christ works in the world.

We can allow ourselves a little smile at Paul's appeal to inter-provincial rivalry with his mention of 'Macedonians', but we do not know enough of the circumstances to be sure what his point is here.

Lastly, read through the passage again, and see if you detect any hints that Paul is here soothing ruffled feathers. People can get very agitated where money is concerned.

Can Paul's teaching in this passage tell us anything about our own giving?

A sudden change of tone

10 1-18 I myself, Paul, beg you, through the meekness and gentleness of Christ, I who am 'humble face to face' among you, but 'courageous when absent' with regard to you. I implore you that, when I am present, I won't [have to] be courageous with the confidence which I reckon on [in order] to face down certain people who reckon that we are operating in a merely human way.

For although we may behave in a merely human way, our strategy is not merely human: for the weapons [we use in] our military campaign are not merely human, but powerful, and on God's side, able to destroy fortresses: [they can] demolish sophistries, and every high tower that is raised up against the knowledge of God. And [they can] take prisoner every intellectual concept, to make it obey Christ; and they remain at the ready, to avenge all disobedience, whenever your obedience is fulfilled.

Look at what is staring you in the face. If a person is confident in himself or herself that they belong to Christ, let them consider this fact for themselves, that just as they [may] belong to Christ, so also do we. For if I start boasting a little too extravagantly about this authority of ours which the Lord gave us (for upbuilding, and not for destruction), I shan't be embarrassed. [I don't want] to seem as if I'm [trying to] terrify you through the 'Letters'. Because someone says, '[Paul's] letters are weighty and powerful, but his physical presence is unimpressive and his rhetoric contemptible.' Someone like that should reckon that we are just the same when present, and in action, as we are at long distance, and by letter.

We wouldn't have the nerve to put ourselves in the same class or compare ourselves to those who 'commend themselves'; but those people who measure themselves by their own standards, and compare themselves with one another, don't understand. We, however, won't boast outside the proper measure. No – our boasting will be in accordance with the measure of the rule that God apportioned to us as our measure, to reach as far as you. For we are not over-extending ourselves, as though we had not reached you; for we were actually the first to reach as far as you in [preaching] the gospel of Christ. You see, we don't boast inappropriately about the work that others have done; our expectation is that as your faith grows it has increased [according to our measure], so that it overflows to preach the gospel in the regions that are beyond you, not to boast about someone else's work in places which are already evangelised. 'Let the one who boasts, boast in the Lord.' For it's not the person who 'commends himself' who is trustworthy, but the one whom the Lord commends.

There is a very sudden change of tone at the beginning of Chapter 10. Paul once again seems very cross, and it is not absolutely clear to the reader what he is cross about. This has led some scholars to argue that Chapters 10 and 11 are part of another letter that Paul sent to Corinth. We shall read it as it stands – but the reader should note that as it stands it is hard to be quite sure precisely what Paul is saying, except that in the final paragraph it looks as though some of his opponents in Corinth have been 'boasting inappropriately', and perhaps claiming Paul's work of evangelising as their own. Paul may well be quoting from what his Corinthian opponents have been saying about him. That is why 'humble face to face' and 'courageous when absent' are printed in inverted commas.

Compare different translations of the last few sentences of this passage, to get a feel of the difficulties in knowing what he was saying. The alert reader will have noticed several words that are important in both 1 and 2 Corinthians: 'upbuilding', 'beg/comfort', 'reckon', 'rhetoric', 'commend'. Some, perhaps all, of these words are clearly 'on the table' between Paul and his Corinthians, but without hearing both sides of the discussion, we cannot say more than that. Notice, too, his reference to 'sophistries'. Paul's readers or listeners in Corinth would have known all about these: the empty cleverness of skilled rhetoricians, intended to bolster weak arguments.

Why do you think that Paul's tone has changed so suddenly?

Don't abandon the gospel

11 1-4 If only you would put up with me, with a little bit of my foolishness! No – please put up with me. For I am jealous for you with the jealousy of God; I betrothed you to one husband, to present you to Christ as a chaste virgin. But I'm afraid that perhaps as the snake cheated Eve in its wickedness, it may corrupt your minds away from the simplicity and chastity that lead to Christ. For if anyone comes and proclaims a Jesus different from the one whom we proclaimed, or if you receive a Spirit different from the one you [originally] received, or a gospel different from the one you [originally] accepted, you put up with it quite easily.

It now becomes clearer why Paul is cross; other Christian evangelists have been disparaging his work, never a wise thing to do with Paul, and arguing that he has preached 'the wrong gospel'. But he does not tell us exactly what the disagreement was about; the Corinthians obviously knew, and he did not expect us to be reading the material two millennia later. So we should be careful not to embrace too enthusiastically all the scholarly attempts to construct a picture of Paul's opponents.

Do you find it encouraging that early Christians squabbled in this way?

Paul is very cross

5-11 You see, I reckon that I am no way inferior to the 'Superapostles'. I may be untrained in rhetoric – but not in knowledge; in every respect we have made it plain to you, in every way. Or did I commit a sin by humbling myself so that you might be raised on high, when as a free gift I preached to you the gospel of God? I robbed other churches when I accepted wages in order to support my ministry to you, and when I came to you and was in need, I didn't burden anyone. For the Christians who came from Macedonia supplied my needs, and [so] in every respect I kept myself from being a burden to you. And I shall continue to do so. It is the truth of Christ in me: this 'boasting' will not be silenced for me in the whole region of Achaia. Why? Because I don't love you? God knows . . .

There is sarcasm here, and we can only dimly reconstruct the charges that had been laid against Paul. Clearly, however, someone else has been at work in Corinth. See the reference to 'Superapostles' and to Paul's lack of training, as well as the earlier references to a 'different gospel', and his insistence on not being supported by the Church he was evangelising. Once again, Paul mentions 'Macedonia' to the Corinthians, possibly meaning his generous (and much-loved) Philippians. For Paul everything always comes back to Christ and to God.

Why is it a problem that Paul preached without charge to the Corinthians?

Testing for fake apostles

12-15 That is what I do – and what I shall continue to do – in order to remove the opportunity (from those who desire an opportunity) for them to be regarded as just like us. For people like that are fake apostles, dishonest workmen disguised as apostles of Christ. And no wonder – for Satan himself disguises himself as an angel of light. So it is nothing extraordinary if his ministers disguise themselves as ministers of righteousness. Their end will be in accordance with the work they have done.

Now we can see more clearly what has been going on. Some people in Corinth have been alleging that Paul wasn't a proper apostle, possibly because he had persecuted the Church, or because he had never known Jesus; but there was also a problem, apparently: he had not been charging for his services (perhaps making rather a point of this), but then asked them to give him money for Jerusalem. Trust between the Apostle and this most prominent of all his churches was at an all-time low. Notice, however, that he turns the argument back on his opponents: it is **they**, *not Paul, who are the 'fake apostles'!*

Paul's 'boasting'

11[16–]12[13] Again, I say, don't let anyone imagine me to be a fool. Otherwise you must accept me as a fool; let me too boast for a little while. What I am saying, I am not saying in the way of the Lord, but as it were as an example of foolishness, in boastful self-assurance. Since many people are boasting in a human way, I'm going to boast, too. For you people, who are so wise, gladly put up with fools. For you put up with it if someone enslaves you, or if someone eats you up, or captures you, or puts on airs, or hits you in the face! To my shame, I must confess that we were indeed weak.

If someone has courage (I am speaking out of foolishness), I have courage also.

Are they Hebrews? I am, too.

Are they Israelites? I too.

Are they descended from Abraham? I too.

Are they ministers of Christ? I am, and more [than that]. (I am speaking as though I were out of my mind!)

My labours have been more [than theirs]; I have spent more time in prison; I have been flogged far more often; often in mortal danger. Five times I got forty-minus-one from the Jews; three times I was beaten with rods; once they stoned me; three times I have been shipwrecked: I have spent twenty-four hours out in the deep. Often I have had road journeys, threatened by rivers, by muggers, by my own people, by Gentiles; threatened in the city and in the desert and at sea, threatened by fake Christians, with hard work and heavy labour, often going without sleep; hungry and thirsty, often going without food; cold and without clothes.

And apart from everything else, there is my daily preoccupation, my care for all the churches. Who is weak, and I am not weak? Who is affronted, and I am not blazing?

If boasting is the name of the game, then I'm going to boast of things to do with my weakness.

The God and Father of the Lord Jesus knows, blessed be he for ever, that I am not lying: [once], at Damascus, the governor of King Aretas was guarding the city of the Damascenes, to arrest me, and I was let down through a window in the wall in a basket, and escaped his hands!

Boasting is the name of the game; it serves no good purpose, but I'll come to 'visions and revelations of the Lord'.

I know a man in Christ fourteen years ago (in the body? I don't know. Outside the body? I don't know, God knows). [Anyway] a person like this was snatched up as far as the third heaven. And I know a person like this (in the body? out of the body? I don't know, God knows); he was snatched up into paradise, and he heard unspeakable words, which it is not permissible for a human to utter.

I'll boast of a person like that; but I'll only boast about myself in regard to my weaknesses. You see, if I should wish to boast, I shan't be a fool, for I shall be telling the truth. But I am being lenient; I don't want anyone to reckon any more of me than what he sees of me, or what he knows from [my lips]. And because the revelations were so exceptional, so that I shouldn't get elated, there was given me a 'thorn in the flesh', an 'angel of Satan' to batter me, so that I shouldn't get elated. With regard to this I three times begged the Lord that it would go away, and he told me, 'My grace is enough for you – for power is made perfect in weakness.' So I shall most gladly boast of my weaknesses, that Christ's power may come to rest on me. So I'm content with weaknesses, insults, torture, persecutions and difficulties, for Christ's sake. For when I am weak, then I am powerful.

What a fool I've been! You forced me! For I should have been recommended by ***you***! For I'm no way inferior to the Superapostles, even if I'm nothing! The 'apostolic signs' were worked among you, in all patience: signs, and portents, and miracles. How did you come off second-best to all the other churches? Was it just that I wasn't a 'burden' to you? Forgive me the monstrous injustice!

We are inevitably rather taken aback by this. What has happened to Paul? He seems to have lost his temper, and to be indulging in some savage sarcasm, and perhaps (as he says in self-accusation) some 'foolish boasting'.

We have to focus on Paul's main purpose in life: he lives, breathes and sleeps Jesus Christ, and anything that takes people away from Christ, especially people who put themselves above the gospel, sends him into a fury.

We can be grateful, however, to the people who were causing so much trouble in Corinth. Without them we should know far less about 'a day in the life of an apostle of Christ'!

Why is Paul boasting here, and what is he boasting of?

Paul's apostolic instincts

14-18 Look! This is now the third time that I'm all ready to come to you, and I shan't be a 'burden': I'm not after what belongs to you – it's ***you*** I'm after! Children shouldn't have to save up for their parents: no – it's parents who should save up for their children! As for me, I'll cheerfully spend – yes, and be utterly spent – for the sake of your lives. If I love you so intensely, am I to be loved any the less? All right – I didn't weigh you down; but I'm a crafty fellow, and got you by a trick. Was it one of those I sent to you? Was it through him that I defrauded you? I begged Titus, and I sent the Christian along with him. Was it Titus that defrauded you? Didn't we walk in the same Spirit? And along the same path?

Once again, the Corinthians know more than we do of what was going on here, and they aren't saying; but evidently Paul has been charged with some kind of deceit; possibly someone had accused him of stealing the money intended for Jerusalem. Clearly, though, Paul is certain that as soon as they think about it they won't believe the accusations, whatever they were.

What kind of a relationship do you detect between Paul and his Corinthians?

A final warning

19-21 Do you think that we have been a long time making our defence to you? We are speaking before God, and in Christ, and everything, my dear ones, in order to build you up; for I'm afraid that when I come I'll find you not quite what I want you to be, and you'll find me not quite what you want. I don't want strife and fanaticism, and outbursts of anger, and outbreaks of selfishness, acts of defamation and tittle-tattle, instances of being 'puffed up', and examples of unruliness. My fear is that when I come back, God will humble me in your presence, and I shall be mourning for many of those who committed sins earlier, and who did not repent of impurity and sexual immorality and debauchery that they had committed.

Paul is clearly fearful that things have gone dreadfully wrong here among his Corinthian Christians. It looks as though some of what has gone wrong is sexual misbehaviour, although that might be no more than a metaphor for not living a godly life. Whatever precisely they have got wrong, the situation requires urgent remedy.

What do you think has gone wrong in Corinth?

Paul's final crack of the whip

13 1-10 This is now the third time that I'm coming to you; 'every legal matter shall be substantiated on the evidence of two witnesses or three'. I have said it before, and now I am saying it in advance of my visit, as when I was present on the second occasion, so now in my absence, to those who committed sins earlier, and to all the rest, that if I come I shall not be lenient again, since you are looking for proof that Christ is speaking in me: he is not 'weak' with regard to you, but powerful among you. For he was crucified in weakness, but lives in the power of God. For we are also 'weak' in him – and we shall show ourselves very much alive with him in the power of God with regard to you.

Examine ***yourselves***, to see if you are still in the faith; test ***yourselves***. Or do you not recognise that Jesus Christ is among you? Unless, that is, you fail the examination. I hope that you will realise that ***we*** are not failures. But I pray to God to do you no evil, not so that we may be shown to have passed the examination, but so that ***you*** may do what is right, and ***we*** may fail the test. For we can do nothing against the truth; we can only act on the side of truth. You see, we rejoice whenever we are 'weak', and whenever you are strong. What we are praying for is your restoration to perfection. That is why I am writing these things while I am away from you, so that when I am present I may not have to deal severely [with you], in accordance with the authority that the Lord gave me (for upbuilding, not for destruction).

Paul is operating in legal mode here; the quotation at the beginning is from Deuteronomic law about valid evidence: 'two or three witnesses' is here adapted into 'two or three visits', and he wants to make sure that there is no evidence of misbehaviour when he next comes – or else! But he is not just playing authority games, like a schoolmaster who fears that he is losing control; see how, as always, he comes back to God-in-Christ and to the Resurrection. The Corinthians (or some of them) have been making accusations against him; in return he forcefully argues that they should look in the mirror and put the accusations to themselves, not so that he can punish them, but so that he can avoid punishing them.

The contrast between 'present' and 'absent' in this section is a deliberate reference to certain criticisms that his opponents in Corinth have been making. But it also goes back to the beginning of this section of the letter (if it is indeed a part of the letter as a whole), and forms an 'inclusion' with it.

What does Paul mean when he says 'Jesus Christ is among you'?

Final (and unusually curt) greetings

11-13 For the rest, my brothers and sisters, be glad, mend your ways, and think the same [as each other], keep the peace, and the God of love and peace will be with you. Greet one another with a holy kiss. All the saints greet you.

The grace of the Lord Jesus Christ, and the love of God, and the communion of the Holy Spirit be with all of you.

With a degree of (perhaps relieved) exhaustion we come to the close of a letter which has maintained its tension – and our attention – right to the end. It is an uncharacteristically brief closing salutation, perhaps indicating how cross Paul is with the Corinthians. This 'postlude' pulls together many of the themes of Paul's correspondence with this difficult and divided community. It is a beautiful and providential irony that one of the loveliest and best-known of New Testament prayers, the 'Grace', with its Trinitarian echoes, is the closing sentence of this tempestuous epistle.

Maps

Palestine of the New Testament
Herod's Fortress
Tyre
Caesarea Philippi (Paneas)
SYRO-PHOENICIA
Trachonitis
Lake Huleh
Cadas
Gaulanitis
Batanea
GALILEE
Gischala
Ptolemais (Akko)
Chorazin
Bethsaida-Julias
Capernaum
Gennesaret
Dion
Magdala
Sea of Galilee
Gergesa
Mt Carmel
Tiberias
Abila
Cana
Asochis
Sepphoris
Nazareth
R. Yarmuk
Mt Tabor
Dora
Plain of Esdraelon
Nain
Crocodilon
THE GREAT SEA
Caesarea Maritima
DECAPOLIS
Pella
SAMARIA
Aenon
R. Jordan
Plain of Sharon
Sebaste (Samaria)
Gerasa
Mt Ebal
Sychar
Mt Gerizim
R. Jabbok
PERAEA
Antipatris
Jaffa
Gadara
Arimathaea
Philadelphia
Lydda
Ephraim
Jamnia
Jericho
Betharamphtha
Emmaus
Jerusalem
Bethpage
Ein-Kerem
Bethany
Qumran
Azotus
JUDAEA
Bethlehem
Ashkelon
Marisa
Bethsura
Gaza
Hebron
Dead Sea
En-gedi
R. Arnon
NABATAEAN KINGDOM
IDUMAEA
Masada

MACEDONIA
THRACE
BITHYNIA & PONTUS
Thessalonica
Amphipolis
Philippi
Neapolis
Apollonia
Beroea
Larisa
Troas
Assos
ASIA
PHRYGIA
GALATIA
CAPPADOCIA
Smyrna
Ephesus
Antioch
Iconium
Lystra
LYCAONIA
Derbe
Tarsus
PISIDIA
PAMPHYLIA
Perga
Attalia
CILICIA
Seleucia
Antioch
SYRIA
SICILY
Athens
Corinth
Cenchreae
ACHAIA
Miletus
Patara
MALTA
RHODES
THE GREAT SEA
CRETE
CYPRUS
Salamis
Paphos
Tyre
Ptolemais
Caesarea
Jerusalem
NABATAEA
EGYPT
Paul's first journey
Paul's second journey
Paul's third journey

NOTES